William Radcliffe

Ellan Vannin

Sketches of the History, the People, the Language, and Scenery of the Isle of Man

William Radcliffe

Ellan Vannin

Sketches of the History, the People, the Language, and Scenery of the Isle of Man

ISBN/EAN: 9783744725569

Printed in Europe, USA, Canada, Australia, Japan

Cover: Foto ©ninafisch / pixelio.de

More available books at **www.hansebooks.com**

ELLAN VANNIN:

SKETCHES OF THE HISTORY, THE PEOPLE, THE

LANGUAGE, AND SCENERY OF THE

ISLE OF MAN.

BY

REV. W. T. RADCLIFFE.

London:

CHARLES H. KELLY, 2, CASTLE ST., CITY RD., E.C.,
AND 66, PATERNOSTER ROW, E.C.

1895.

TO THE

MANX PEOPLE,

BY THEIR FELLOW COUNTRYMAN,

THE AUTHOR.

CONTENTS.

CHAP.		PAGE
I.	THE UNRECORDED AGES.	9
II.	HISTORIC TRACES	15
III.	AGES DIMLY SEEN: DRUIDIC AND EARLY CHRISTIAN.	21
IV.	AGES DIMLY SEEN — (*continued*): RUNIC AND PAPAL	31
V.	ELLAN VANNIN: PAST AND PRESENT	39
VI.	THE MANX PEOPLE: CHARACTERISTICS, RACE, AND LANGUAGE.	49
VII.	THE MANX PEOPLE: CHARACTERISTICS (*continued*)—PROVERBS AND SUPERSTITIONS	59
VIII.	MANX FREEDOM: THE NEED.	71
IX.	MANX FREEDOM: THE PROGRESS	87
X.	MANX WEALTH: HINDRANCES	95
XI.	MANX WEALTH: HELPS AND SOURCES	107
XII.	SOCIAL CHANGES: TRANSITION FROM ROMANISM	119
XIII.	SOCIAL CHANGES: THE ESTABLISHED CHURCH	127
XIV.	SOCIAL CHANGES: MANX METHODISM	139
XV.	SUMMARY AND REVIEW.	153

ILLUSTRATIONS.

	PAGE
DOUGLAS .	*Frontispiece*
THE STONE CIRCLE .	10
ST. MICHAEL'S, LANGNESS	14
MAUGHOLD	16
OLD FORT, LANGNESS	20
BALLAGLAS ROAD	22
PEEL CASTLE	32
GLEN COAN, GROUDLE	40
HANGO HILL	48
INJEBRECK RIVER	50
CASTLE RUSHEN, CASTLETOWN	60
BALLURE CHAPEL	72
TYNWALD HILL	88
THOLT-E-WILL BRIDGE	96
RAMSEY	108
RUSHEN ABBEY	120
BISHOP'S COURT	128
WESLEYAN CHAPEL, SULBY GLEN	140
LAXEY GLEN	154

PREFACE.

THE design and special feature of these pages may be noted as a summary of the History of the Manx People from the early ages to the present. The fabulous and the doubtful are omitted. The external events are recorded only as related to the central idea of the book. The research necessary has demanded an area of wide extent and much care in statement. The valuable volumes of the Manx Society, the Histories of Governor Walpole and of Train, the useful Guides, the Manx Note Book, and other local sources—the Manx ruins included —have been laid under contribution, with a grateful acknowledgment which the writer would now record. In addition, he may mention the Manx Dictionaries of Kelly and Cregeen, the *Memorials of the Derby Family* by Seacombe, the writings of Patrick, the works of Bede, Dean Murray's *Irish Church*, Bishop Lightfoot's *Leaders in the Northern Church*, Canon Wright's *History of the Early English Church*, the Lecture on St. Patrick by Rev. W. T. Hobson, M.A., the recent pamphlet on Early Manx History by Rev. T. Talbot, the Biographies of Bishop Wilson by Stowell and Keble ; collateral Histories of England, Scotland, and Ireland, such as by Dr. Smith of Cornwall, Wylie, and, for more general purposes, Green and Gibbon ; other works, ecclesiastical and secular, giving incidental light on Manx topics, have been passed in review. The reference to volume and page was at one time intended, but abandoned in the interest of simplicity and economy. The writer has had in view his Manx fellow-countrymen as his chief readers, and specially the young people of the Island ; at the same time he hopes that the visitor will not find the volume too exacting, but, on the contrary, helpful in glen and upland and ancient ruin, on Snaefell with its grand panorama, or sailing round the rock-bound shores from the Calf to the Point of Ayre and their connecting lines east and west. An area of thirty miles by twelve in the midst of a vast continent might easily pass without notice, but the same area fixed in the Gulf Stream, where Ellan Vannin has its position, or elsewhere in the ocean, strangely becomes more important and suggestive. The Island is but a rock in the centre of the British Empire, too small to belong to itself, too feeble to resist invasion, too isolated to share quickly in general external progress, but its historic interest is uncommon. The ocean storms around have helped its beauty and grandeur. Its solitude has left it rich in ancient ruins, guarded by a useful superstition; its nearness to other lands has given it a place in collateral history, specially of Britain, Ireland, and Scandinavia; its language, still on the printed page, though falling into disuse, remains without material change from past ages, though the languages of England and of lands once in the Roman Empire have been lost in modern developments; its form of government comes from a more remote antiquity than that of any neighbouring kingdom; its liberties have been won without violent revolution; its evangelical religion has triumphed without the blood of martyrs; its prosperity has grown from conspicuous poverty into a degree which, with not many of distinguished wealth, leaves few without money, and those few generally too independent to be paupers. The country, the people, the progress in freedom, wealth, morals, religion, and social life, form a subject of unusual interest. The position of a Manxman in his native land is richly historic, with glimpses of the neighbouring countries and of European affairs in the remote past, and he owes it to himself to know what he may of Ellan Vannin. Immediately around him are monuments and institutions which recall two thousand years. It is hoped by the writer that these pages may have something to interest the youth of his native Island, and that, perhaps, wandering across the sea, they may remind a Manxman of the land he and his fathers have left behind.

W. T. R.

P.S.—I am indebted to the kindness of Mr. Dean, photographer, Finch Road, Douglas, for most of the illustrations, which have been selected from his admirable collection of Manx scenes.

1895.

The Unrecorded Ages.

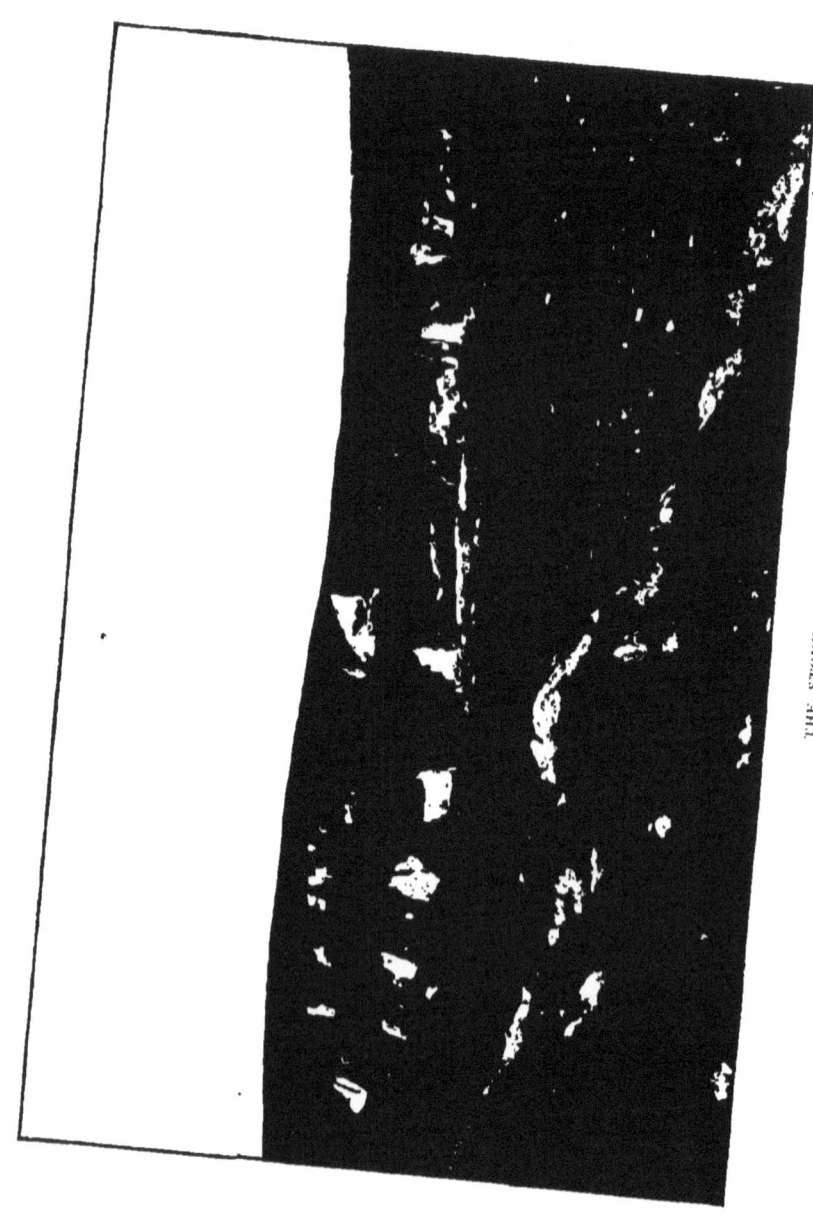

THE STONE CIRCLE.

ELLAN VANNIN.

CHAPTER I.

THE UNRECORDED AGES.

FOR about a thousand years of the Christian era, we have but little that is authentic for Manx history. Much related is simply fabulous; much is without adequate evidence. Under the former may be classed the mists of "Manninan Mac Lear," the miracles of St. Patrick in the Island, the adventures of St Maughold in his coracle from Ireland to Maughold Head, and some other marvels of the same class. Considerable confusion as to alleged facts has been caused by the confounding of the two Monas, the Welsh Anglesey and the Manx Man. In a communication to a Welsh friend of mine, Professor Rhys writes that "Manxmen seem to have forgotten that there was a Welsh Mona as well as a Manx Mona," and that they have "confounded the history of the Welsh island with the Manx island." He adds, "This, I am told, is the explanation of the assertion that a dynasty of Welsh princes ruled over Man. The conquest of Man by Edwin rests, I believe, on two passages in Bede's *Hist. Eccles.*, ch. v. and ix., where he mentions, among the Englishman's conquests, Menavias Insulas. This has easily been supposed to mean Anglesey and Man, but I am by no means sure that

Man is included." Adequate historic evidence seems to require the exclusion of much that some have held to be true in relation to the Druids and their connection with Man. In a pamphlet by the Rev. T. Talbot, of Douglas, the point is dealt with in the light of the knowledge of an expert in Manx history, and their presence in Man he regards as without evidence. What has often been assumed as true of St. Patrick in Man, seems to belong to the same category of things doubtful. In his autobiography, published by the Religious Tract Society in its Christian Classic Series, and under the editorship of the Rev. C. H. H. Wright, D.D., St. Patrick never mentions the Island, and in the record of his life leaves no room for a Manx mission and episcopate. The question has been ably argued in the negative in a pamphlet by the Rev. W. T. Hobson, M.A., of Douglas; but further remarks must be reserved for a later chapter. Edwin of Northumbria ruled from Edinburgh, south and west, over a large strip of England as well as Anglesey, but there is no proof of sway over Man.

The list of the Bishops of Man falls under the same remarks as to want of evidence; and the line of Welsh rulers; and things alleged of the earlier of the ages deemed Scandinavian. The list of the early Bishops did not appear in print until about 1671. The monks of Rushen, in their *Chronicle*, say nothing of the Druids, nothing of King Orry and his dynasty, and nothing of Bishops until the time of Godred Crovan, in and after 1077, when they mention Roolwer as Bishop. And that chronicle is taken to date from about 1250, its record beginning at 1065, and is the earliest reliable account of the Island. The earliest history is in 1482; it contains the oldest map of the Island, with the outlines of the ancient lakes. "The supposed original *Chronicle of the Isle of Man*," professing to go on to the time of the Revestment in 1765, is not of much help in the history. The parish registers give no light; with the exception of Ballaugh in 1598, they are not earlier than the seventeenth century, the period of Chaloner's history, Bishop Wilson's coming a little later, and beginning its account at the Norwegian conquest, with no notice of a Bishop until 1151. Thus blank are the days of old.

The dearth of historic material may be explained in part. It is not entirely peculiar to Man. The early light on British history comes from its place in the empire of Imperial Rome. It was the same with other nations, the Huns, the Goths, the Vandals, Lombards, and Franks; their early history is not from themselves, but from the annals of the great empire. Manxland was not within that empire. Tacitus relates that Agricola, with his forces, reached the Grampian range of Caledonia, but the little Island not far away on his left, was outside of his sphere. When Ireland had the fame of Christian culture, and Scotland had its Iona, the Manx Mona from its obscurity was not seen. Few wrote history in those ages. The monk Gildas, as a writer of British history, seems to stand alone, between 449 and 607, and he writes chiefly about Kent and the Saxon invaders. Writing itself was rare. The laws of Saxon England were in writing until about 600; those of Man, not until 1422; and, in the Manx language, no Book until 1709.

There were also special causes for the dearth in Man. The successive transfers of the Island would imperil historic documents, and the various invasions; Mary, daughter of Reginald, in her escape, might remove some of the Manx records; and yet more, the Countess of Derby, when she left amid the troubles of the Commonwealth. Sacheverell states, in his history, that some of the early Christian records of Man might be destroyed in the Papal ages to avoid the comparison of more modern corruptions of the truth with the earlier purity; just as the early annals of Iona were destroyed under a decree of the Popish Synod of Argyle.

The historic light reaches Man just as the Scandinavian comes to plunder the "little nation," which even in the time of Bede was not supposed to number more than three hundred families.

ST. MICHAEL'S, LANGNESS.

Historic Traces.

MAUGHOLD

CHAPTER II.

HISTORIC TRACES.

NE of these is the *Norse invasions.* They have left their impress on Man, just as they did on Shetland and Orkney and the Hebrides, on their southern course to Britain and the Irish Sea. The Island then was held as a "Norwegian Principality." The conquest of it by Godred Crovan at the battle of Sky Hill, in 1077, stands connected with his escape from the Norwegian defeat at Stamford Bridge by the English King in 1066, the same who, later in that year, fell at Hastings before William the Conqueror. The list of Godred's successors included Reginald (1229), Olaf (1237), Harold (1248), the last of the dynasty being Magnus (1265). The Scotch supremacy followed under Alexander III., who changed the arms of Man from the Norwegian ship to the Three legs. The Manx kingdom was "Man and the Isles" until 1156. On the conquest of "the Isles" by Somerled, it became simply "Man." Early in the thirteenth century Reginald had surrendered it to the Pope. Leaving the marks of these violent times, let us go to the ages of *early Christianity* in the ruins of the Treen Chapels. These are traces of a happier memory. They may belong, perhaps, to the age of St. Ninian at Whithorne, when he laboured within sight of the Island, and will be considered in the next chapter. Earlier than these, some of the ruins have been deemed Druidic. Next, come the Runic memorials, after the early

Christian, and found chiefly in the churchyards. Lastly, we have the Romanist ruins, most conspicuous of all, and of which a summary may here be given. Chief among them is the Cathedral on the Islet of Peel, with its five acres of land and rock, anciently termed "Holme," a term signifying, according to Canon Bright, of Oxford, in his work on *The Early English Church*, ground surrounded or washed by a river. The tower near the Cathedral is not unlike the round towers of Ireland. The outline of the Cathedral may be easily traced, chancel, nave, and the prison beneath suggestive of the "moddey dhoo." There are also the ruins of official residences and of erections for military defence. Dating from about 1134, in their foundation, are the ruins of Rushen Abbey, once belonging to Furness Abbey, but less extensive than the ruins on the islet. A few fragments remain of the Friary in Arbory. In Kirk Michael, Bishop's Court stands in its own domain. The Nunnery, near Douglas, has a few ruins where, two centuries ago, were remains of some extent and importance. The old churches, mostly of humble structure, and St. Trinion's, must also be included. To these traces in ruins must be added some which may be termed literary. They are partly in the ancient laws, partly in the Manx language itself, as it bears the marks of its historic course. The Manx "Carvals," though an interesting feature, belong to later times ; they are a literature of themselves, rich in correct Manx, and, if not of a high order in poetry, are characteristic, and have been of central interest when sung in the "Oie 'l verry"; the solitary singer with his MS. in hand, and a lighted candle, and words of his own choice, all bearing the memory of Romish times. Under the head of "literary," the publications of the Manx Society are entitled to a foremost place. Of course, all are not of equal merit: Feltham's tour was hastily written and lacks research; Waldron's volume abounds in the fabulous; and Camden admits the absurd, as when he states that Manx women never went abroad but in their winding-sheets, and that only one sheep in a flock was "loughtin" in colour. Then there are the traces of surviving civil institutions, in wh ch the "Tynwald" is chief, and full of suggestions of the past. The Tynwald Court represents a system of government more ancient in its basis than the English House of Commons with its date of 1264 in the reign of Henry III. Its Norwegian origin appears on the surface; according to Professor Munch it means "a field for Parliament." It is assumed to have been founded by King Orry; it includes the "Kair as feed," the twenty-four members of the House of Keys, of whom eight, when it was "Man and the Isles," represented the Hebrides, and has as essential members the Council and the Governor—who presides. The proccedings of the annual assembly, on each July 5th, are full of Manx history which looks back to the time of Scandinavian conquest, while it now tells of constitutional freedom. With all their value, however, these historic traces leave much untold of a long interval, and of much bearing on the condition of the Manx people in the ages now long past, while the modern annals abound in interest.

OLD FORT, LANGNESS.

Ages Dimly Seen: Druidic and Early Christian.

BALLAGLASS ROAD, NEAR RAMSEY.

CHAPTER III.

AGES DIMLY SEEN: DRUIDIC AND EARLY CHRISTIAN.

E have seen that, in the ancient ruins and surviving institutions and laws, will be found the alphabet and elements of Manx history. The island is rich in such memorials. At the same time it may be noted that none of the ruins suggest Wales, and there is nothing of Imperial Rome. The Romans never came nearer than Galloway, on the opposite coast of Scotland.

1. *Druidic Ages.*—Were there such in Man? In the Welsh Mona, of course, all admit the idea; but how as to the Manx Mona? Professor Rhys, as has been noted, is of opinion that the two Monas have been confounded, and some may hold that the Druidism credited to the Manx Mona really belonged to the Welsh.

On the affirmative side of the proposition, which asserts a Druidic period in Man, are such arguments as these:

Druidism was the religion of the Celtic race two thousand years before the Christian era, though it had no place south of the Alps, or east of the Rhine, or in the lands between the Adriatic and the Tigris; or, east of a line having Germany on its west, from the Mediterranean to Scandinavia. But Gaul and Britain and, though less conspicuously, Ireland, were its home; and Man, within a few miles, with a people of the same race and language as the greater islands, was not unlikely to come under the power of the same system. The expulsion of the Druids from

Anglesey in the year 59 of our era, by the Imperial forces, might naturally lead them to seek refuge in the other Mona, which was not far away. The more intimate relations of Man to Ireland might suggest the same thought of probability; for, as late as 636, the Druidic pretender had contended with Donald, the Christian king, for the crown of Ulster, according to an Irish account of the time. In the Manx language, again, are found terms in which the Druidic idea is suggested; as ."Glendarragh," the oak glen. Manx has the word for Druid, "Druaight." The English word "enchanters," in Jeremiah xxvii. 9, in the Authorised Version, is, in the Manx version, "Druaightee." Dr. Kelly states in his Manx Dictionary that "Laa yn Ullick," Christmas day, means the day of the mistletoe (uil or guil=mistletoe), the sacred plant of the Druid. The *Enc. Brit.*, in its article on Druidism, states that Baal worship, with its fire, was a part of its ritual. "Laa Boaldyn," according to Cregeen, May day, contains a reference to the fires (teine) of May eve, the term "Belthane" being also used for the same fires, meaning, as is stated by Dr. Kelly, Baal's fire. The "Oie Vaaltin" of the eve of May day, was the night of Baal's fire. In years which some have not yet forgotten, the line of fire was still kindled along the heights of the island. "Tinvael" is the fire of Baal. The "breast law" of the Druid finds its parallel in the "breast law" of Man before the laws were written, as also in the Brehon laws of Ireland. In "Hunt the wren" on St. Stephen's day is the sacred bird of the Druid, in Manx termed "Dreain," the feathers supposed to have special virtue. Ruins at Mount Murray, Bellown, Spanish Head, Cregneash, Port Soderick, and the Cooil, not to name others, have been taken as Druidic, and Druidism in the island has been admitted as a fact by the general authorship on Manx history.

On the other hand, some may doubt the force of such

inductive considerations. There is no Druidic life, as still in Wales which has its Arch Druid, and no trace of the traditional mental culture, unless it be in the knowledge of the medicinal properties of herbs, in charms still spoken of, and in devices by which witchcraft may be defeated.

If the system ever had a place in the Manx Mona, it did little for the elevation of the people. With the soul's immortality, it held the soul's transmigration, the worship of Baal, and human sacrifices. The oak forest, the unhewn stone circle open to the skies, the central stone for the human sacrifice, the auguries, omens, and incantations, the huge image of wickerwork with its crowded victims, the great festivals in May and November, would be a terror not a power to uplift. Bondage to the priesthood held the system together. At fixed times the fires must be kindled from his sacred flame, the smoke drifting over the fields believed to be a protection of the crops and cattle from witchcraft, because from the fires of Belthane.

On the whole, some might hold that the alleged ruins are wanting in the specific marks of Druidism, and that it was late in the centuries (about the sixteenth) before any writer favoured a Druidic era. Still some shadows of the system seem to linger in Man, in thought, language, and memorials; and some probabilities remain with the thought that it is not unnatural that the religion of Britain and Ireland, in the pre-Christian ages, was the religion of people of the same race and language in Man.

2. The "Treen Chapels" touch the times of *early Christianity* in the island.

The term "Treen" seems borrowed from later times, and implies an ecclesiastical and parish organisation of great completeness for the tithes of the Church, such as could not have obtained a place among the simple, early structures whose ruins evidently belong to an age when that arrangement did not exist. In Cregeen's Dictionary the "Treen" is defined to be an arrangement which divided the tithes into three parts. One-third was for Rushen Abbey; the remaining two-thirds were divided between the Bishop and the parish clergy.

Each "Treen" was a group of "quarterlands," by which the Island was broken up as a basis for taxation for both civil and church purposes. The parish arrangement was also an element, for to each of the seventeen parishes were allotted ten Treens: each Treen forty quarterlands; the whole Island being thus measured into 680 quarterlands. The Treen, in its taxation, had a threefold reference to Bishop, Abbey, and parish clergy; it was therefore after and for these organisations in chief.

The Treens are not mentioned by the monks of Rushen Abbey, who have indeed left without notice all things ecclesiastical for more than a thousand years. The Abbey lands seem to have been before the time of the Treens, for there are no Treens in them, though they include so much land. The quarterlands were mapped out before the parishes; for some of them extend into more than one parish, while they differ also in size. The Chapels did not belong to the time of parishes, but to a previous age. The full arrangement designated by the term Treen agrees better with the middle ages of Manx Romanism. The parish idea did not come early into the Celtic Church. In Ireland, as late as the eighth century, there were, in the modern sense, no parishes, and no dioceses; and Man, so closely related to Ireland, would not be likely to be in advance in its church plans. The term Treen therefore seems to have its origin in the later and better ordered times, while the Chapel precedes the setting up of parishes. It may have been at first used as a convenient term of description for ruins which were of old. The Treens are still a basis for taxation in the civil and ecclesiastical; they are still manorial divisions of the land, with a charge for the church as well as for the lord of the manor. A Manx friend informs me that his farm of 140 acres is assessed to the lord's rent as three-fourths of a Treen, and that the Moar, in collecting the yearly sum for the rent, also demands a curious item termed "Prescriptions," for the church, in lieu of an old tithe charge for the farmer's live stock and the poultry of the farmyard.

The character of these Chapels points to the early ages in the dawn. On an average, they are twenty feet by ten, with space for about twenty adults, a door at one end and a window at the other, east and west; constructed of wood and earth; sometimes with burial-ground around; rectangular in outline; and with nothing of the solid masonry of later ages as at St. Ninian's and the Islet of Peel. Their number, from the ruins, was considerable. At Nappin, in Jurby, on to the south; "Lag ny Keillen," the glen of the churches; "Cronk ny ira laa," the hill of the rising day; St. Michael's Isle; ruins at Mount Rule, Laxey, Port St. Mary, and many other places, are the outlines in ruins of these ancient structures distributed through the Island. Belonging to the ages of early British Christianity there are similar structures in England, Scotland, and Ireland. Canon Bright, in his work on *The Early English Church*, tells of such in Scotland and Ireland built of wood, or of wattles plastered with clay, with a roof of thatch. There were some such in Galloway in the fourth century, in the Highlands of Scotland, and in the Hebrides. Their style is noticed by the poet Wordsworth at the grave of Rob Roy. The "Candida Casa" of Ninian, the church of white stone, which gave its name to Whithorne, was an exception in its time. The more substantial and stately belonged to the later Romish period.

These Chapels, therefore, fit into collateral history and into the early ages of British Christianity. Within the first four centuries British Christianity was in the fulness of its energy. In his *Religion of Early Britain* Dr. George Smith deems it probable that Christianity reached Britain in the Apostolic age, noting specially his own county of Cornwall, in its relations to the Eastern lands, near to Judea, relations of commerce with marks of Christianity in the early centuries. Tertullian writes, in the second century, that the Gospel had reached some parts of Britain which had not been conquered by imperial Rome. British Christianity, in 314, had its representatives in the Council of Arles; and, in 325, in the Council of Nice. In the Dioclesian persecution, from 303 to 310, British Christians had sought refuge in Cornwall, in Wales, and in the northern parts near the Solway, almost inaccessible to the Roman power. It is thus that the Celtic, and not the Roman, Christianity marks the early ages in the British Islands. It was a power of resistance to the monks of Augustine. It sent forth from the Irish Bangor, for example, missionaries to Cornwall, in the early evangelisation, who, in passing down the Irish Sea within sight of Man, would not forget their kinsmen on the little island. St. Bees, also, was not far off, on the edge of Cumberland; nor Whithorne, at the Mull of Galloway. Canon Bright relates that, in 597, Augustine found the ruins of British churches which had been destroyed by the invading Anglo-Saxons. Before 597, Rome had no church position in these lands. St. Alban, St. Patrick, Columba, Columbanus, and many other great names, belonged to another fellowship. The last, with his helpers from Iona, led on the mission to France, south and east; and so, from and after 612, was Christian truth disseminated in Germany, in Switzerland, and across the Alps into Lombardy. There is evidence that the Irish Bangor held its theology free from Roman interference in the seventh century. The successor of Augustine complained that the Irish Bishop would not eat with a Bishop from Rome, as is recorded by the Venerable Bede. Not only from Ireland, and places already named, was there near Christian light; but perhaps, not the least from the Mull of Galloway where Ninian, in 370, had his school of training for young evangelists who, as they rose early in the winter for their studies, as tradition says, could see the lights of the early risers on the opposite shore. The outer ecclesiastical Baronies, with their independent jurisdiction and powers in the legislature, may have grown out of the simple relations of missions to the Manx people in the earlier ages.

The position of Bangor and Sabal in this circle of Christian zeal was conspicuous in other directions also. Under Columba, the Irish evangelist in the sixth century (born 521), and who had Iona as his centre, the men trained for Christian service were sent to labour among the Picts and Scots, from about the year 563. From Iona, Aidan, himself Irish, was sent to be Bishop of Lindisfarne, with the Saxon kingdom of Northumbria as his diocese. He had to lay aside his Irish speech and learn the Saxon for his new sphere, while the king, meanwhile, often acted as his interpreter. It was a warm stream issuing at first from the coast of Erin round to Northumbria by the line of Iona, and had relations to Man as well. The circumstances of British Christianity from the fourth to the seventh centuries coincide with the theory of an early Christianity in Man during the same interval. The records of the Middle Ages make no mention of these Treen Chapels; they had then probably fallen into ruin and were forgotten. They belonged to the class of "rural oratories" of which Bede writes in his time, and which served the outlying hamlets of England in the seventh and eighth centuries; "quarter-land oratories," as Cumming terms them, and at a period before England submitted to the Papacy in 664, and long ages before Ireland submitted in 1172.* The modern Irish patriot, as he glories in the ancient fame of his country for Christian culture and civilisation, is apt to forget that, whatever might be its value, it belonged to the ages before 1172. To that interval the Christianity of Man belonged also.

---

* The "Treen" arrangement does not seem to belong to the "Chapel" era; it was part of a system of taxation for Bishop, Abbey, and Clergy towards the Middle Ages. The Christianity of the "Chapel" ages was no part of the Papal system. The time of absorption by Romanism is not certain; but it was, perhaps, after the Norwegian conquest, when we read of royal gifts to the clergy, and of the Island itself to the Pope.

Ages Dimly Seen (continued): Runic and Papal.

PEEL CASTLE.

CHAPTER IV.

AGES DIMLY SEEN (CONTINUED): RUNIC AND PAPAL.

3. THE *Runic remains* are chiefly stone monuments, with the symbol of the Cross, set up by one friend in memory of someone else, and inscribed with "runes," or letters of the Runic alphabet, whose twenty-four letters served the literature of Scandinavia of old. They are cut in deep, straight lines, long and short, on the edges of the stones. The Runic language was that of Scandinavia, and included the peoples of Norway, Sweden, and Denmark. It was closely related to the Gothic language. Gibbon states, in his *Decline and Fall*, that the oldest runic inscriptions are supposed to belong to the third century, and that the first ancient writer who mentions the runic crosses lived towards the end of the sixth century. In order of time, the runic remains follow the early Christian of the Treen Chapels, and belong to the Norwegian era, which begins about the ninth century. The *Encyclopædia Britannica* states that about the tenth and eleventh centuries the Runic letters gave place to the Roman. The monuments are found, perhaps, more in the north of the Island than in the south. They relate to persons of Norse descent and name. There is no expression of Christian sentiment in what they bear, unless it be in one of which my friend, Mr. Kneale, of Victoria Street, Douglas, informs me, and which has the words "for his soul." They are not now in their original sites; some are built

into other structures, some carefully placed in churchyards. Their date is supposed to be about the tent century.

The Runic interval seems to have been a passing phase rather than a substantial change in the religious life of the Island. It points to Norwegian supremacy. Iceland shares in the same kind of memorial, basaltic columns bearing the runic inscriptions. On the lines of more general history, it suggests the great movement of the northern nations of Europe to take possession of the fairer lands of the sunny south. The date when the movement reached England, Ireland, and Man, has been stated by Professor Manch to be from 800 to 850. The Manx kingdom was then "Man and the Isles." In England, the Norsemen seized Cumberland and Strathclyde, the western half of Britain from the latitude of Edinburgh to that of York, and from the northern boundary of Wales to the Clyde. In 882, on the eastern coast, the Danes had subdued Northumberland, and had made York their capital. In Ireland, the Norwegians had formed a kingdom in Dublin, taking possession also of Waterford and Limerick. A little earlier the Norwegians had conquered Shetland, the Orkneys, and the Sudreys, the last including the western islands of Scotland and Man. These western islands, as south of Norway, received the name "Sodorenses," a term at last joined to "Man." It suggests the possible origin of the title, "Sodor and Man," given to the Manx diocese, in which case the ancient "Sodor" would be "the Isles," now included in "Argyle and the Isles," and would, as the more important part, naturally come first; thus, "Sodor and Man." The great northern movement which thus reached our little Island was, in its general features, a repetition of the more ancient movement of Goth, Vandal, and Scythian, before whom the Roman empire fell; and of that yet earlier movement from the

RUNIC AND PAPAL AGES.

northern regions down to India, the Dravidian invasion sweeping before it the aborigines of India, to be driven southward in its turn by the Aryans from the north-west. So Gibbon, already referred to, writes that "the men of Scandinavia had been concealed by a veil of impenetrable darkness" in their northern lands, strangely quiet, though, a little south of them, in an earlier age, on the southern line of the Baltic, Goth, Frank, Vandal, and Lombard had left their country to subvert the imperial power of Rome; at last, however, came the Norsemen from their cold recesses to seize Man and greater countries, Normandy as well, and not resting until they had established their power as far south as the Mediterranean. It is a curious fact that recently, on the coast of Norway, a vessel of the "Viking" class, built of oak, has been found embedded in the soft earth, in good preservation, though supposed to be of the ninth century. An exact copy has been built by the Norwegian Government, and sent as a present to the "World's Fair" of 1893, in Chicago. The measurement is: Over all, $76\frac{1}{2}$ feet; beam, $16\frac{1}{4}$ feet; hold, $5\frac{3}{4}$ feet. The bow and stern are higher than amidships. There is no deck; the planks overlap; it is fitted for thirty-two oars, each 17 feet long; and the lines are graceful as those of a modern yacht. Perhaps it was such that once came to Lhen Mooar.

4. *Manx Mediæval Romanism* comes within the ages seen but dimly, though its ruins are the most conspicuous. In the dimness may be seen something of its system, its resources, its government, and its relations.

Its date in Manx History, as an organised church, could not be earlier than the mission of Augustine in 597, but must have been much later. Irish Christianity withstood the Papacy until 1172, as already noted, and Manx Christianity has been more closely related to it than to Scotland or England, and would therefore, under the shelter of Ireland, be free from subjection to Rome to a much later date than England, in 664, at the Synod of Whitby. In order of time, Manx Romanism comes after Manx Christianity. The oak had long grown and flourished before the ivy crept along its branches. The date would be long after the time of St. Patrick, which was about the middle of the fifth century. Many of the fallacies of the Papal system in Man, as elsewhere, gather around the grand personality of St. Patrick. The claim that he laid the foundation of the Church in Man falls for want of historic evidence. Probabilities are against the supposition that he was ever Bishop of Man, or was ever within its bounds. The monks of Rushen Abbey never name him in their chronicle, and state that they had no knowledge of any Bishop in Man before the eleventh century. To them the first thousand years of the Christian era in the Island were a blank in its Church history. In his autobiography, St. Patrick makes no mention of the Island. Born in Dumbarton in 372, the capital of the ancient Strathclyde of British history; taken captive by pirates when he was sixteen years old, and sold into slavery in Ireland; escaping to his British home after ten years of bondage; it was not until some years after his conversion to the Christian faith that he returned to Ireland, and, according to his own account, gave his whole life of Christian labour to Ireland alone. His first landing, we are told in the narrative, was in Ulster, two miles from Sabal, near where now stands Downpatrick. His first sermon there was in a barn, to which was given the name "Sabhal Padrine" (see the volume published by the Religious Tract Society, and edited by the Rev. Dr. Wright), the title meaning the Barn of Patrick. On that site was afterwards erected a memorial church, standing north and south. Of his presence in Man there is no adequate proof or record; none in the writings of Gildas, the monk of the Welsh Bangor, and the historian of the British Church in the sixth century; none in the writings of Bede in the eighth century, though he refers to the Isle of Man; none, therefore, in the early ages, for to these two writers are we indebted for the Christian history of Britain and the neighbouring lands. The first published statement that St. Patrick had been in Man was by the monks of Furness Abbey in 1112, six hundred years after he had passed away; the next mention of the idea is in 1573. In the dark ages there were published lives of St. Patrick full of fabulous inventions, and these have been repeated from age to age. The saint himself never mentions the Island, or Rome, or the Pope, or any commission from Rome, or any miracle by himself. His writings, composed towards the end of his life, have much of the Gospel spirit, and include his celebrated hymn, which he wrote in ancient Irish, the rest of his writings being in imperfect Latin. Had the alleged wonders of a Manx episcopate been real, they could hardly have been omitted from his review of life. One thing seems clear, that the island had no share of his labours, or even his presence; that his achievements had nothing to do with early Manx Christianity; that his British usefulness had no part in laying the foundations of Romanism; that those foundations were different in outline and plan from those of the early ages, and that the ultimate absorption of the Celtic Churches of Britain and Ireland and Man is no proof that they belonged at first to the organisation of the Romish system.

The system of Manx Romanism appears in its ruins, the Cathedral, Bishop's Court of its time, but not now in ruins, the Abbey at Rushen, the Nunnery, the Friary, the Church of St. Ninian's, and old parish churches whose traditions survive; and, lastly, its early relations beyond its immediate circle in the Baronies beyond the sea. Together, these suggest a comprehensive and imposing ecclesiastical plan. Beyond the Baronial relations were those to the Archbishop of Drontheim, in the Norwegian time; to the Pope of Rome, made its master by the usurping king; to the Archbishops of Canterbury and York; to the lord of the isle as, for a time, independent of his authority in their local jurisdictions. The priestly arrogance which thus arose, and refused feudal homage to the Stanley ruler, was quickly put down by a firm hand, those abroad dismissed, those within the island escaping by submission. The discipline and government thus established over the Manx people show Rome's method as a Church. There are words in the Manx language that bear the Papal impress: "Oie innyd" is the special name given to the eve of Ash Wednesday; "Oie 'l varry," "the night of Mary," is Christmas Eve. Places sometimes bear a suggestive name, as "Magher y Chairn," the field of the Lord. It does not appear that the priests used the Manx language in public worship. The Canon Law was in full force; the doctrines were those of the Papacy; the discipline was true to the Romish model; the claim was exclusive, as being the only true Church, and with powers in the priesthood which approached the divine; the supremacy over the civil power held in theory, as was natural to a system whose chief feature is that under the Christian name it aims at political supremacy.

The revenue comprehended large resources: tithes and fees from every property and business, and from the chief events in family life, as well as all the offices of religion; extensive properties in land and houses; other rights and claims of a substantial nature also; and this, not only for insular Popery, but also for the outer establishments. Other facts bearing on Manx Romanism must be reserved for the chapters on "Freedom" and "Wealth."

Ellan Vannin: Past and Present.

GLEN COAN, GROUDLE.

CHAPTER V.

ELLAN VANNIN: PAST AND PRESENT.

BOLD words affirmed, in days when faith was strong
And doubts and scruples seldom teased the brain,
That no adventurous bark had power to gain
These shores, if he approached them bent on wrong;
For suddenly, up-conjured from the main,
Mists rose to hide the land—that search, though long
And eager, might be still pursued in vain.—WORDSWORTH.

E have now passed through the mists in which some real things could not be seen, and in which often some things have been unduly magnified; and we have at last landed on Ellan Vannin, and can see it apart from the fabulous. Much of its history grows out of its geographical position in the northern angle of the Irish Sea, between the 54th and 55th degrees of north latitude, and between the 4th and 5th degrees of west longitude, in the line of the North Channel as it enters the Irish Sea from the Atlantic, almost directly south of the Hebrides along which the Norwegian pirates came on their southern raids. It lies, as if pointing to the Solway Firth, just where the three kingdoms come within sight of each other and of Man. On its west, Ireland is within sight; on its north the Scotch shore round to the Mull of Galloway; on its north-east, Whitehaven, St. Bees, and the mountains of Cumberland; by a line direct towards the north from Kirk Bride, the fields of Scotland show their workers in harvest. The main features of Manx history arise from this central position among greater

countries. It was in the natural course of things that the island should be peopled by the Celtic race near to it on the neighbouring countries, and that those countries should covet its possession; that, small and helpless, it should tempt the violent injustice of the early ages; that, when Christianity triumphed on the shores not distant, Christian zeal should seek the welfare of the little island within sight; that, in the line of the pirates from Scandinavia as they came south, the Manx, as well as the people of the Hebrides, should be plundered and oppressed; that, sheltered in comparative seclusion, its ancient ruins should be among the least disturbed; that, with its climate and attractions, and so easily accessible, it should now be a chief watering place for the peoples around; a climate not so severe in winter, or so oppressive in summer, singularly even in temperature, and in quality for health not inferior to some favoured places in the south of Europe. Plants and flowers elsewhere needing artificial shelter in winter, or cold season, flourish in the mild open air. The sea breezes are everywhere; the atmosphere is full of health; vegetation is rich, and sometimes rare; scenery is varied in form and colour; the free outlines of the fields tell of freeholds and independence of great ownership. The bold outline of the rocky coast agrees with the storms and tidal currents around. The transparent sea is free from the pollution of great rivers with crowded cities and towns on their banks; there is pleasant fishing in stream and sea, and opportunity for searching the rocks for shell-fish. The position of the island is thus an explanation of past and present, and a prophecy of its future. Its Ordnance Survey reports as its area 145,325 acres   (*Blue Book*, 1893, p. 50).

Judging from the oldest map, the island has undergone great changes in outline and interior. On the north-west, it has been worn away by the tidal current that sweeps around

Point of Ayre ; on the north-east, it has gained on the sea : from the "Lhen Mooar," the great lake, to "Carlhane," the crooked lake, there are traces of the channel of the sea which once made Jurby an island. In the interior, there were extensive bogs where remains of the oak forests have been found in the depths, and lakes of which vestiges are still visible. Ballaugh was anciently Ballalough, the last syllable being the Manx for lake. In Lezayre, and Closelake, and Kirk Andreas, and Kirk Bride, were lakes whose marshy lines have not been entirely dried up ; from the Sulby river, across the Regaby road, and towards Ballavoddan, are still traces for a student of the past when what is now land abounded in fish, in which the monks and bishop had an interest. The tenure of the land in some of those parts, I understand, is "Intack," which means that it was once common, as it would be if formerly the bed of a lake. Along the depressed line of road from Douglas to Peel, lakes are marked on the oldest map. At Port e Chee, near Douglas, is the wide area where probably the tide used to spread out beyond the point of meeting where the "Dhoo" (Black), flowing past Kirby, and the "Glass" (Grey) past Port e Chee, blended, and gave to Douglas its name. The idea seems not improbable that, once, the valley between Douglas and Peel was a channel of the sea, making the southern section an island. The skeleton of the Elk, and similar remains, found in the deep turf of the north, tell of a fauna different from the present, when animals of orders now unknown to Man had their place and home within its bounds. To pass from the animal to the human, there are the graves without a history, with inverted urns suggestive of heathen burial, as at Cronk ny Marroo, "the hill of the dead." There are the "Cronks," whose line from the north might be part of a system to telegraph round the Island the news of an invasion from Norway or elsewhere. The cross roads still remain, narrow and steep, that used to shorten the road from Douglas to Ramsey, and in other parts; they were the highways, at last set aside by easier roads, some of which are now superseded by the electric tram.

In the modern changes there has been loss as well as gain to the scenery. The piers, the breakwater, the tower of refuge, in Douglas Bay; the marine drive on the Head, and the improvements at Port Skillion, on the one side; and, on the other, the splendid promenade to the hill of the Burnt Mill, with the electric tram to Laxey and Snaefell as an extension, are all additions to nature's beauty; and yet there is some loss of beauty in having Castle Mona shut in by other buildings, however comely, instead of being alone in grounds extending from Broadway to the ancient dwelling of McCrone, and from the coast line back to the road where the duke's gardener had his cottage in the good old times. To the modern improvements at Douglas should be added those at Ramsey, Peel, Port St. Mary, Port Erin, Laxey, and other places. Obscure recesses, but full of curious beauties, are rapidly opening out, such as Cregneash, which represents the oldest times in Man. The modern advance of agriculture also adds to the scenery as well as the wealth: fields once lying waste are brought under cultivation, and districts unsuited for the plough are planted with trees, a measure which, if fully followed out, would, in the course of years, add much to the resources of the Island.

It may not be easy to define the special attractions of the Island. There is, of course, the sense of seclusion from the whirl of ordinary life in the larger country; there may be the sense of solitude in the quiet recesses by sea, or on mountain range. Besides isolation from the wider world, there is the life-giving atmosphere, the fresh scenery, the pure sea ever near. On each week-day there are the stirring scenes of departure and arrival from the chief places on the opposite coasts of England, Ireland, and Scotland. In addition to the unusual variety of fine scenery, there are the ruins—a study by themselves. To some, no doubt, the sail is a drawback, with liability to storm; but the steamers are among the finest in the home navy of the United Kingdom, and the voyage is not much beyond three hours and a half, and the accommodation, easily obtained, all that reasonableness in charge, courtesy in bearing, and trustworthiness in provision, can make it.

There are three methods of seeing the Island. One is by sailing round it on a fine day, a trip of six hours from Douglas Bay, turning northwards. Along the coast headland and bay alternate, Groudle, Laxey, the Dhoon, Maughold Head, Ramsey. At Ramsey the Bahama Bank, with its flashing light by night, is not far away; King William's Bank also, so named from his narrow escape there from shipwreck on his way to the battle of the Boyne. Then, with glimpses of Scotland on the right hand, the course, bending round Point of Ayre, brings to the north-west, where the brave Elliot, in 1760, defeated the French Squadron under Thurot. Along the west side of the Island rich views rise in succession: the Islet of Peel, with harbour behind; "Purt ny Hinshey," as it used to be named—in English, "The Harbour of the Island"; and just opposite to it, on the sea, the meeting-place of the tidal currents from north and south at "Contrary Head." Farther south projects the rock of Niarbyll, where crabs shelter in good numbers, and Fleshwick Bay; yet grander scenes open next at The Calf, Spanish Head, and Langness; and so, passing Port Soderick, Douglas Bay finishes the excursion.

There is a grander view of the Island from the summit of Snaefell, two thousand feet above the level of the sea, and commanding, at one glance, one of the finest views in the United Kingdom. Immediately under the eye of the spectator is the Island, with its range of mountains from north to south, with many a valley and glen, and an area of 140,985,470 acres of land; beyond the sea are Whitehaven and the mountains of Cumberland, the fields of Scotland, the Mull of Galloway, the mountains of Mourne, and perhaps, if the day be clear, Snowdon—a total extent of prospect of about 3,000 square miles.

But neither the sail nor the ascent should prevent a minute inspection of the inland scenery. I knew a visitor who, becoming specially absorbed in one object, made the view from Snaefell suffice for his sight of the Island. The better method is to take road and rail and walk, to trace the pure streams in the cascades of Glen Helen, Glenmay, Rhenass, the Dhoon, and elsewhere; and to find out in valley and quiet recess the gems of the scene, the rare plants or flowers, the glimpse of the sea, the secluded places, where most of the poetry of the Island will be found.

The authorities of the Island are awake to the importance of guarding public order amid the myriads of visitors from all parts of the kingdom. In such vast gatherings there will naturally be some of the less reputable. The large watering places have seen the necessity, in their own interest if not for higher reasons, of maintaining sufficient police supervision, and that it would be commercially unwise to allow in those who refuse the moral restraints of public decency, what would offend the moral sense of their best customers, and lower the reputation of the place. In a similar course, the authorities, whether in the governor and magistrates, or municipal powers, will not lack the support of an enlightened public opinion in the Island. Such care may drive away the worthless and the profits of their habits of excess, but more than an equivalent will be realised in the well ordered families with their young people, whose moral surroundings will be thus guarded.

One great difference between the present and the past of half a century may be mentioned as to public Sabbath observance. The old times had their defects, but on the Sabbath Douglas, for example, had no shops open, no boating in the bay as now, no excursions by sea, and few by vehicle, no oyster and cigar shops doing business, nor sacred concerts, as some term them, with which to while away the evening hours.

HANGO HILL (*see page* 83).

The Manx People: Characteristics, Race, and Language.

INJEBRECK RIVER.

CHAPTER VI.

THE MANX PEOPLE: CHARACTERISTICS, RACE, AND LANGUAGE.

THE character of a people will generally reflect their ancient history and their physical surroundings. Of none is this more true than of the Manx people. By an ancient writer in the fifth century they are termed "a tribe of Scots." Until the ninth century "Scot" included the Irish. 1. The race is the Celtic. It came, in the distant past, from its Aryan home in the East, and took possession of the countries bounded by the Alps and the Rhine—the ancient Gaul—and spread over Britain, Ireland, Man, and the lesser islands of the west of Europe. The race had two branches—the Cymric, now represented by the Welsh, and the Gallic, now represented by the Irish, the Gaelic of Scotland, and the Manx. The three last have dialects which closely resemble each other, and show the identity of the language; that spoken by the Cymric (the Welsh) is more remote. The four belong to the Aryan group of languages, where also Sanscrit, Zend (the ancient Persian tongue), Greek, Latin, and German have their centre. It has been calculated that only about two-thirds of the Manx language are found in the Manx Scriptures and Prayer-Book. There is something of the Scandinavian in the Manx nature, as might be expected, and as appears in the liking for a seafaring life in a degree not found in the Irish or Welsh or Highland. The Norse rule for three centuries must have led to a mixture of the two races, which perhaps was more in the south than in the north, where Godred Crovan, after his conquest at Sky Hill, allowed the natives to remain, choosing for himself and his followers the southern section of the Island. In the schools of fifty years ago, whatever may be the case now, the study of navigation was a marked feature. The Manx sailor has proved himself to be among the most skilful and daring, and has often risen to the command of the ship on his own stormy coasts and on foreign seas. The sailor into whose arms the wounded Nelson fell at Trafalgar, it is related in an account which I have seen, was a Manxman of the name of Cowle. Less honourable, but true to this Norse feature, is the fact that among the mutineers of the *Bounty* were two Manx sailors, one Christian and a Heywood from the Nunnery. Still, the Manx element in character is supreme. The Anglo-Saxon intermarriages belong mostly to modern days, and there never was an Anglo-Saxon invasion.

The Manx population of the early ages must have been much reduced by savage invasions and insular conflicts. The number given in Bede's time was 300 families, say 1,500 persons. This was in the early years of the eighth century. Eight hundred years after, in 1584, the Manx numbered only about 4,800. In the first decade of this century the numbers had risen to 34,316, in the second to about 40,000, of whom about 20,000 spoke Manx; now the census amounts to 55,608.

The emigration to England, the Colonies, and the United States of America during the last seventy years has been considerable. In Liverpool and Manchester the Manx have held annual gatherings. In South Africa and the Australasian Colonies many of them have found a home; in the United States, yet more, especially in Ohio. In the

CHARACTERISTICS, RACE, AND LANGUAGE. 53

wider competition which this implies success has not failed, in commerce, in science, in government, in the professions, in literature; it would be easy to give names typical in the several branches. The Manx and their descendants abroad, added to those within the island home, would raise the total number thousands above the insular census.

The Celtic prefix "Mac" was once common in Manx names, and told of the Celtic origin of the people. In 1408, nearly all the clergy of the island had this prefix, and in 1417 sixteen of the twenty-four Keys. The many names with the initial C and K show the last letter of the original Mac which has been allowed to lapse.

2. From race let us proceed to language, as to which the writer admits that in half a century he has colloquially forgotten much. In the region of Gaul, Spain and Italy, the original Latin of the Roman empire has been broken into the modern languages of the succeeding kingdoms. The Celtic, however, retained its hold in western and south-western Britain, and, of course, in Ireland and Man, which were never a part of that empire. Dr. Blair remarks that Celtic is one of the oldest among the languages of the world. It was at one time the language of ancient Gaul, northern Italy, the western parts of continental Europe bounded by the Rhine, as well as that of the British islands. Celtic history, which begins about the sixth century, includes the two great sections of the race, as already indicated, with the addition to the Welsh of Cornish and Armoric, the last being the language of Brittany in France. Manx is essentially what the Celtic was at first when Ireland and Scotland were peopled by that race. Irish, Gaelic and Manx can easily understand each other. Strangely, on the contrary, modern English

has become what the sixth century could not understand. Saxon and Norman-French invasion accounts for the fact. The surrounding sea in part accounts for the unchanged character of Manx. Some of its terms are singularly suggestive: for "child" the word is "lhiannoo," half a saint; "lhiabbee," a bed, is half food or life. "Balla" stands for a town or an estate: "Sheading" includes the term for six, and denotes the six political divisions of Man. "Treen" denotes a division of land with tithes divided into three parts. In terms which express the theological or what relates to the Church, it is indebted to the original languages of Scripture almost entirely. In things sacred, it has a peculiar dignity in expression, of which, to the Manx ear, the last phrase in the Apostles' Creed is an example in the resounding swell of "y vea dy bragh farraghtin," the life everlasting. It has words to express the sublime distinctions of the Athanasian Creed. It can rise to the heights of the Te Deum and to the strains of *Paradise Lost* in Milton. Its resources now are best found in the Manx Bible. In specific terms, it is not abundant; the genus has to be united to the various species often with a rather rough effect, instead of some more elegant specific word, as generally in English. In a Manx sonnet on the cuckoo, the word for its call is "gerrym," which means also the crowing of the cock. In the proverb on the divine approval of one poor man helping another poor man, the word means "laughter" for joy. Verbs are sometimes wanting as one Manx idiom may illustrate: In the Manx Prayer-Book, the clergyman does not say "let us pray" as it is in English, but "let us take prayer," "lhig diun padjer y gooiall." There is a term for a gift over and above what was bargained for, "dooragh": "warp" and "tallee" express the three herrings followed by one more, as the fisherman counts his herrings by the hundred. When a gang of workers is so arranged that one of them is always resting, there is a word to describe the man who rests. There is no term for slave; the nearest approach to it is "stoudaystey," one required by government to work for less than the usual wages. Besides words from Hebrew and Greek, there are some from Latin, and, as might be expected, from Scandinavian, or more definitely, Norwegian and Danish, and many from English. "Qualtagh" denotes the first person you meet in the new year. In the terminations ness, ick, ell, ay, ey, as in Langness, Ronaldsway, Snaefell, Soderick, Laxey, Ramsey, we have the Norwegian; in those ending in "by" as in Jurby and Colby, we have Danish. Some of the personal names are common to both Ireland and Man. It has been thought probable that the old spelling of the language has been lost in the ages when it was only spoken and not written. The present spelling seems to have been formed from the sound in speaking, and to date from the time of the Manx translation of the Scriptures. The etymology, it is said, is best understood by comparison with the kindred dialects. While the writer notes the features of the language with diffidence, from the long years that have passed since he was fairly familiar with it, he has pleasure in referring to Cregeen's Introduction to his Manx Dictionary, where the Manx student will find a useful summary of knowledge of the language. He remarks that the structure of the language, viewed grammatically, conveys the idea of elaborate culture in its "texture and beauty," and notes its subtle changes in initial letters, "in moods and tenses, and regards it as like a piece of exquisite network, interwoven together in a masterly manner, equal to the composition of the most learned, and not the production of chance. The depth of meaning that abounds in many of the words must be conspicuous to every person versed in the language."

Manx is purest in the north. Unlike English, it generally has the noun before the adjective. The "black horse" in English is the "horse black," "cabbyl dhoo," in Manx. There is a singular exception to this rule in the adjectiv "drough," bad, or evil, which is before the noun in the designation of Satan as the evil spirit, "drogh spirrid," and of bad women as "drough varrane" in the famous old "Carval." The differences between the dialects are less to the ear than to the eye. A Manx friend of mine could easily understand a sermon in Gaelic which he heard in Scotland. The Manx Fencible, when on guard in Ireland in the later years of the last century, easily understood the whisper of one Irishman to another, as they stealthily approached to attack him—"cur daa," "give it him," was Manx as well as Irish, and put the soldier ready for defence. It has been suggested by an article in the *Encyclopædia Britannica* that the difference of the Manx dialect from the other two has arisen from the isolation of the Manx people under Norwegian rule. In the earlier third of this century Manx was generally the language of the labouring class and of the farmhouse, and it had its separate and regular services at Church and Chapel. Of the words in the language fifty-nine per cent. are Manx, twenty-one per cent. Norwegian, and twenty per cent. English in origin, with traces of Greek, Latin, and Hebrew.

Manx literature is within narrow limits. Its first book, printed and published in 1709, was the Catechism of Bishop Wilson, the translation by Cowley from the Bishop's English. The Manx Bible, the Manx Prayer-Book, the Manx Hymn-Book, translated chiefly by Killey, the Dictionaries of Dr. Kelly and Cregeen, a part of *Paradise Lost*, translated by Christian, of Marown, some religious tracts, are among the principal works in the native tongue.

A list of works in Manx may be found in Vol. II. of the issue of the Manx Society.

The Manx had close relations with Scotland and Ireland. The language was but slightly different in dialect from what was spoken at Bangor, Sabal, Iona, and Whithorne, and all were moved by the same religious life. The closest relation, perhaps, was with the Irish.

The Manx People: Characteristics (continued)
—Proverbs and Superstitions.

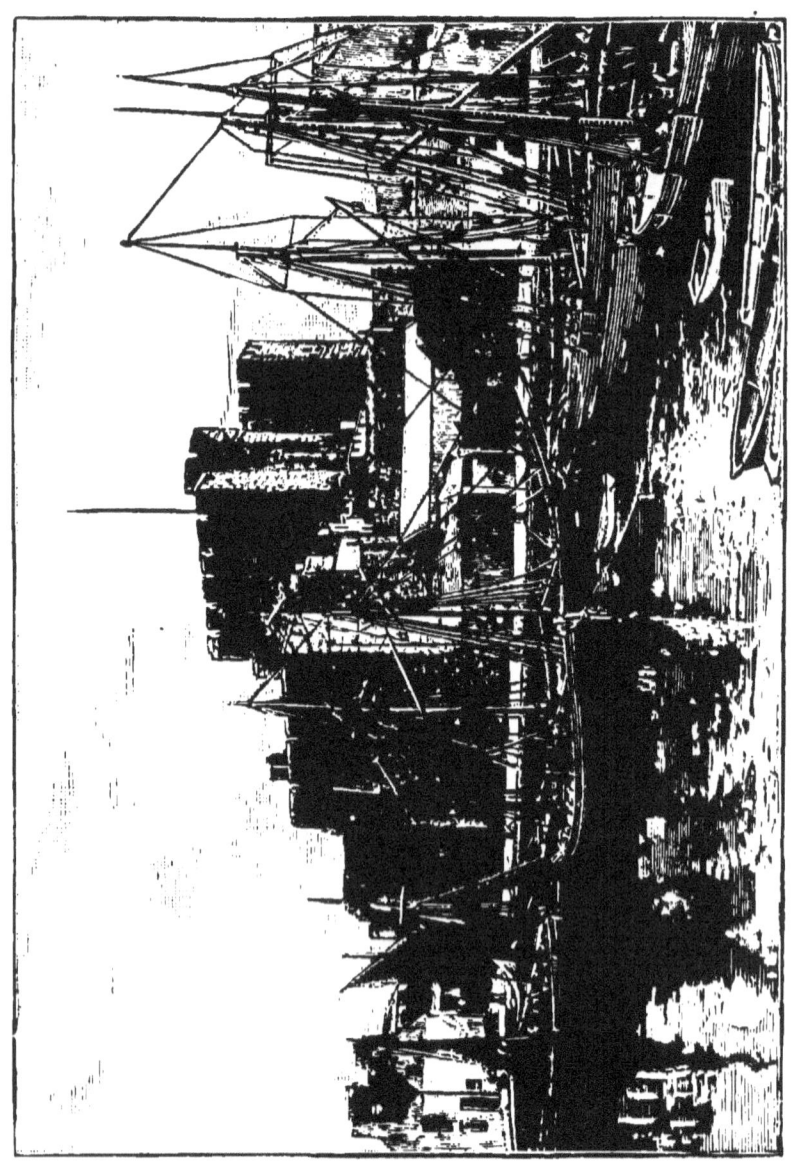
CASTLE RUSHEN, CASTLETOWN, ISLE OF MAN.

CHAPTER VII.

THE MANX PEOPLE: CHARACTERISTICS (CONTINUED)—
PROVERBS AND SUPERSTITIONS.

3. IN the proverbs of a people will be found much of their natural character; they suggest the maxims and ideal of their life; they are, in fact, the result of inductive observations, general conclusions drawn from many instances for future wisdom. In this case it is the proverbs without surrounding literature.

Their general character is homely common-sense, often expressed in metaphors drawn from the ancient quiet life, and with a tone of depression and discouragement. In some there is an excess of caution bordering on want of energy, with little of the adventurous or speculative, and perhaps undue emphasis on the wisdom of making haste slowly. In some are great principles and noble thoughts, the value of learning, the beauty of benevolence, the vanity of shams; the superiority of moral excellence to the merely intellectual, and of the real to the plausible, are enshrined in some; in others, homage is paid to wisdom, to economy, to industry, contentment, temperance, and responsibility in life, and the government of the tongue. There is nothing of the selfish, though a full share of the prudent. "Take care of number one" has no place among them. They advise against undue elation in prosperity, and urge the value of humility and reality in character; they don't omit kindness to animals. A good selection of the Manx proverbs may be gathered from the Manx Dictionary of Cregeen. It may interest some to see the original Manx with the English in a few examples:

Ta'n aghaue veg shuyr da'n aghaue vooar.
The little hemlock (evil or sin) is sister to the great hemlock.

Boght, boght dy bragh.
Poor, poor for ever.

Foddee yn moddey s'jerree tayrtyn y mwagh.
Perhaps the last dog may catch the hare.

Ta ynsagh coamrey stoamy yn dooinney berchagh, ast'eh berchys y dooinney boght.

Learning is the comely clothing of the rich man, and the riches of the man who is poor.

Cha vel eh laccal gergagh ta goaill soylley jeh aigney boriagh.
He will not lack comfort who takes the enjoyment of a contented mind.

Ta dooinney creeney mennick jannoo jeh e noid.
A wise man often makes a friend of an enemy.

Foddee fastyr grennagh ve ec moghrey bodjelagh.
Perhaps there may be a sunny afternoon after a cloudy morning.

I add a few in the English translation:

A green hill when far from me; bare, bare, when near.
After spring tide comes a neap.
The smaller the company, the greater the share.
Change of work is rest.
The crooked bannock straightens the body.
Don't tell me what I was; tell me what I am.
Give a piece to a raven, and he will come again.
To take is sweet; but to pay is better.

There are many more proverbs, given in various publications; and there are many sayings with much of the proverb in them, though not quite so terse as the proverb is. On the whole the Manx proverbs answer to much found in the Manx character.

4. Manx superstition is not less interesting than the Manx proverbs. It is not easy to define superstition; the

term is often used so indefinitely as to include much that does not belong to the subject. Belief in the spiritual world of Scripture is not superstition, nor is belief in the relations of that world to this. Superstition is "a corrupt rite," as some writer has said. It may be taken as a system of corrupt rites. It has its primary sphere in false religions; it seeks to corrupt what is true. The former is seen in heathenism, past and present; the latter in the fallen churches of Christianity. In its rites and ceremonies its range extends from the ridiculous to the terrible. It is a perverted belief in things supernatural.

Nations generally have their superstitions. Egypt had its magicians; Chaldea its astrologers and sorcerers; the Israelites were warned against using enchantments and dealing with familiar spirits. There have been forms of divination in Greece and Rome by serpents, by clouds, by the flight of birds and other ways, and elaborate systems associated full of folly and cruelty and corruption. So among the nations at large.

Take England. In one of his papers in *The Spectator*, Addison remarks that "there was not a village in England that had not a ghost in it; that the churchyards were haunted; that every large common had a circle for fairies belonging to it; that there was scarce a shepherd to be met with who had not seen a spirit." Carleton, in his *Traits and Stories of the Irish Peasantry*, does justice to the same feature in that land of the Celt. Hugh Miller, in his *Schools and Schoolmasters*, is equally rich in what relates to the kindred superstitions of Scotland.

The Isle of Man shares the same features, and naturally enough, for the people are of the same race and, because isolated, more liable to the full force of the system. At the same time, it seems only just to add that there has not been the extreme superstition which Waldron represents in what he wrote about the Island, and who was apparently more expert in his office in arresting smugglers than in gathering from the natives the facts of Manx superstition.

In their source some of the superstitions are Celtic, some Norwegian, some from the Romanism of the Middle Ages. I will attempt a partial enumeration of the wild ideas. To begin with, there is, according to some, the removal of the Island from Lough Neagh, in the north of Ireland, both still about the same size and form. Then there are the mists by which Manninan Mac Lear hid the Island from his enemies. In connection with the sea, the floating island, the mermaid, and many a mysterious scene under the ocean are mentioned. One, at least, is amphibious—the Tarroo Ushtey (water bull), who emerges occasionally from lough or river, and who used to make some timid as they passed the Lhen Mooar. The most mischievous are the Fairies, who ride on cushags at night, carry off some people for a time, are angry if they find the farmhouse without bread on their nightly visits, and show it by dashing the spoons and knives and forks from the box hanging up in the kitchen on to the table; and still, though the noise was heard, the knives, etc., were found in their old place in the morning. The Boganes are numerous, causing some fear in certain fields and houses, but useful in preventing people from being out too late at night. Only one moddey dhoo (black dog) has been noted, that in the Bishop's dungeon at Peel. It is difficult to describe two others —the Glashtin and the Lhiannan shee, the first a goblin, the second a familiar spirit. The giant among them all is the Phynnodderee, a hairy satyr of great strength, and of kind temper if kindly treated; one who can thresh a stack of corn (a "tooran") in a night for the farmer. Of the unseen crowd who have sometimes embarrassed a man's movement in the dark in a lonely road on his way home, perhaps after he has had some "jough" refreshment, I am unable to speak, but I have been told of great difficulty in getting free. There are signs also—the forerunners of the wedding, the baptism, the funeral.

In a somewhat different line are the supernatural things connected with individuals. St. Patrick, in his fight with the giant at Peel, and in his service to the Island in driving every venomous creature out of it as he did to Ireland, and other wonders; and St. Maughold, manacled in his coracle, and floating from Ireland to Maughold Head, where the key to unlock the manacles was found in the mouth of a fish. There is also the roofless church of St. Trinion's, the "Keil Brish" (broken church) near Crosby, and on which somehow no roof would remain, the Phynnodderee having to do with the difficulty.

Leaving these, we come to things yet more strange; for the creatures named have not been seen in later times; but there are spells, charms, herbal manipulations, remedies for what has come from the evil eye, and from ill-will, witchcraft defeated. Marvellous cures, too, are spoken of, after consultation with the wise man, and stories are told not easily explained. Worthy people will tell of things weird and far from the natural course of affairs in life; illness has followed the invasion of some ancient ruin, and has passed away after an approach to restitution, when the removed stone has been returned, and the disturbed ruin, where the plough has come too near, has been re-adjusted. For untold generations, the mound in the "Garee" has remained unopened and covered with gorse, an unexplained mystery of the past; the cows which had strangely failed to give milk, have at length, after prescribed rites, been restored to their usual course; the churning which had failed to produce butter has succeeded after due use has been made of the dust swept from the path of the evil wisher; the disease fatal to the poultry has been arrested by mysterious methods; the bleeding which defied all effort to stop it, has yielded to the will of some one to whom the case has been stated. So some of us have been told by some of ancient Manx intelligence and belief in such affairs, and have been left almost unable to solve or deny.

How Manx life has been touched by the Manx superstition is an interesting study to one who investigates the condition of the Manx people, present and past. Within the first third of this nineteenth century the fairies had not ceased their alleged interferences; the character of the "Qualtagh," the first you meet in the new year, was of far-reaching influence. On long winter evenings, in the semicircle fronting the kitchen fire, there has at times been a kind of rehearsal among friends and neighbours, giving a summary of the wonderful times long gone; and as each has moved nearer to the fire, with ears quick to hear any unusual sound, and with a deepening interest in the supernatural, the youngsters present have feared to go to bed in the dark, while others have not been free from apprehension as to what might happen on their lonely walk home after all the "coosh" of the evening.

In this general survey of Manx superstition, it is evidently a vanishing quantity : it resembles a decaying empire losing province after province. If in the remote times there was Druidic superstition, with its sanguinary terrors, its occult meanings from the angle at which the human victim fell at the stroke of the Druid's knife, its omens and auguries from the entrails — this has left no vestige behind it : if the superstitions of the Romish ages once had sway, so as to demand the civil power for the suppression of some of them after the Reformation, these also are gone, whether connected with Patrick, or Maughold, or holy wells, leaving the Manx people the most Protestant of the Protestants of the British Empire, in doctrine as well as superstition. It may be added that the part of the superstition relating to the unreal hierarchy from fairy to phynnodderee has also vanished. The rest is passing, though here and there belief lingers, perhaps, in the virtue of the charm and in the midnight ritual of herbs. Of the extreme veneration for the old ruins one cannot speak severely, for it has much to do with their preservation.

The general effect of superstition does not make for dignity of character; it looks away from the divine; it holds the human as wielding a supernatural power; it glances towards the infernal; it touches life with imaginary terrors; it leads to hope from occult powers when the refuge should be common-sense, science, and religion. The effect is the loss of dignity to the individual and the community. Other and higher influences, however, prevented the natural results.

It will be seen that my definition of the superstitious does not include belief in ghosts, though this is sometimes superstition because imaginary. The scepticism of the ages has ever been unwilling to admit the ghostly, because, admitted, it is logically fatal to its argument. The superstitious stands apart from the spiritual world revealed in the Scriptures, generally unseen, but with evidences of reality sometimes in startling forms, as in the scene of Endor in which Samuel appears, and as in that on the holy mount where Moses and Elias were seen by the disciples. To accept the reality of ghostly appearances, with the marks of accustomed authenticity, is not superstition. Baxter, Wesley, and other great writers of the Christian past have held to that position. Hugh Miller was no enthusiast, and those who have read his *Schools and Schoolmasters*, and his work on the English people, will remember, among other admissions, his assent to the ghost story in the time of the second Lord Littleton, in 1779, at Hagley. One of the most gifted ministers I ever knew, and author of one of the grandest theological works of the age, once told me of his refusal to lodge in a certain room allotted to him in his first Circuit, because of what he held to be a well authenticated story from the lips of his friend who had been an eye witness. On the other hand, there has been, no doubt, undue belief in this sphere among the Manx people, and with comic effects. I know a churchyard in the north of the Island where occurred a scene like the following: A man of the parish, when not quite sober, was apt to call at night at the grave of a former debtor with the request that the debt might be paid. A wag of the village adjacent, and whose name I could give, hid himself one night in the church porch, ready with his white sheet to make a ghostly appearance if the creditor came; on arrival, somewhat "fresh," the being in white emerged, but the creditor would not wait for his money, and escaping over the stile, sought refuge in the village, where it was found that fright had made him sober.

There are great abiding characteristics, amid the lesser features mentioned, arising from the historic past. One of these is a robust Protestantism with a broad toleration. The idea of the Popish past and the strong position of evangelical religion are the explanation. Anglican tendencies have little Manx sympathy. High Church ideals do not succeed. The same prevalence of evangelical light will account for the absence of popular scepticism, whether in the form of the old infidelity, or Darwinian evolution, or the so-called Higher Criticism. Between the Evangelical Churches and the Sunday-schools of the Island and the sound principles generally held by the population, the truths to which England owes its greatness and freedom prevail.

The loyalty to the British throne of the Manx people is equally conspicuous. There is something of local government in the functions of Tynwald, but it exists under a reserve of supreme power which fails to strike attention because of the wise moderation of both the government and the governed. It is nothing like the Home Rule proposed for Ireland. In contrast to that country, the diffused ownership of the land has much power. Few areas of thirty miles by twelve in the United Kingdom can show so many freeholds, and these, for the most part, continued by inheritance. The kind of social distress which is often revolutionary does not exist. There is no overcrowding of the population as in the Scotch Highlands and the West of Ireland. There has long been the emigration which comes from enterprise to the United Kingdom and its colonies and the United States of America. There is no undue pressure of population upon resources. The loyalty is firm in its basis in the Manx character which is not given to change, and offers the fewest chances to the anarchist. The spirit that does homage to just law has had its life in the influence of Manx Christianity. Even under the old system of tithes, I have seen parson and farmer on the best terms in the harvest field, when each tenth "stook" of the crop was marked off for the church, and the trying law obeyed. The rebellion against the revival of tithes in the potato and green crop in the time of Bishop Murray was an exception in Manx temper; the claim had been generously given up by Bishop Wilson, and ceased from his time. Loyal submission to the law of the land has been, and is, a chief feature.

Manx Freedom: The Need.

BALLURE CHAPEL.

CHAPTER VIII.

MANX FREEDOM : THE NEED.

THE government of the early ages is but little known. We can find no historic signs of freedom. If we assume a time of Druidic rule, it would be oppressive to the last degree. The interval sometimes allotted to the sway of Edwin of Northumbria, and others, in the obscure ages, if held to be authentic, would not relieve the scene. The government of the Norwegians, from Orry to Godred Crovan, and from Godred to the last of his line, when the Scots came into power, was that of invaders and conquerors, who robbed the Manx people of their rights. In all those ages the general condition was exposure to violence. Under the Stanleys the spirit of the government was feudal, and the reverse of free. The offering of a brace of falcons at each coronation was, to Manxmen, a sign of arbitrary power. In the Institution of Tynwald liberty was possible rather than real. In theory, there was the authority of the "Commons and Tenants of Man," but in fact there was no power to control or modify the ruling policy. Tynwald, with its fence and security, as the alleged meaning of the word would suggest, left the people without freedom. Under the title of "The Commons of Man" had been united, with the House of Keys, at times, six representatives from each sheading, and four from each parish; sometimes mention is made of a "Court of the whole country." These met once at Reneurling in Kk.

Michael, once at Castle Rushen, and once at St. John's but the ruling power was really a tyranny, and liberty only a name. The monks of Rushen speak of "The Sheriff of Man"; a similar official is named in *The History of the Hebrides*, but his powers cannot be defined. It is said that Reginald, son of Godred, "King of the Isles," was chosen King of Man, in 1187, by the Manx people; but if so, the historic circumstances show that the case was really invasion and conquest. From the time of Orry, usually fixed at about 912, to the time of the House of Athol, no substantial freedom can be found. There seem to be traces of a dual government on each side of the mountain range, with some difference in the laws. Tynwald was held at Keill Abban, in Baldwin, in 1429, and in other years at Cronk Urleigh and Castle Rushen. Since 1577, it has been held at St. John's, "Cronk y Keillown," as termed in Manx, "the Hill of St. John's Church." Until the time of the Stanleys, little is known of the House of Keys, and then there was no due recognition of popular rights. The people were treated as a mere appendage to the land, not to leave the island without government permission. Even after the sixteen members for Man had been increased by the eight for "the Isles," the "Kair as fead" had but little power. The same disregard for Manx rights prevailed, more or less, on to 1662, when in defiance of law and right, the life of "Iliam Dhone" (brown William) was taken at Hango Hill. Liberty could find no place under the "breast laws" of the earlier centuries, under the ecclesiastical Barons, under the Papal ascendency, under the Canon law, under a self-elected House of Keys, with a co-ordinate Lord of the Isle.

There were other dominating influences, also, unfavourable to freedom. Until the Revestment of the Island in the British Crown, in 1765, there was no imperial refuge from local oppression. Before the gift of the Island to Stanley by Henry IV., England had long won its Magna Charta, but Man was a stranger to the liberties then asserted. Invasion, violence, usurpation, injustice, with no relief from the Norwegian, and but little from the Scots, had sent their accumulated evils into comparatively modern times. The isolated position, limited population, the too patient Manx submission, left the people to the often unjust sway of the lords of Derby and Athol.

In the distant past, the frequent change in the lordship of the Island had hindered freedom. In 1219, Reginald had surrendered the island to the Pope, so giving him the appointment of the Bishop, the control of ecclesiastical affairs, and the power of Canon law in the Manx diocese. The separate jurisdiction of the ecclesiastical Barons, with their independent courts, the Bishop with his prison at Peel, as well, added to the bondage. In such an environment, true liberty could not exist. Then came the transfers afterwards, when Norway retired; to Scotland in 1252; to the Earl of Salisbury in 1344; to the Earl of Wiltshire in 1394: to the Earl of Northumberland in 1402. Norway still coveted its former position as late as 1238; Edward I. and his successors advanced claims, and Scotland disputed about possession. The Island became an imperial prison for the Earl of Warwick, in Peel Castle, in 1398, and for the Duchess of Gloucester in 1446. The expert seamanship and bravery had been enlisted by English sovereigns against the pirates who infested the Irish Sea; but the service brought no amelioration to the Manx people.

The peculiar position and character of the Derby rulers was a barrier to Manx liberty. The family historian, Seacombe, unconsciously relates much of what was adverse in their training and habits. The times of Henry IV. did not understand the rights of man. He had seized the English throne from his cousin, Richard II., in 1399, and, to secure Church support in his usurpation, had promised to crush the Lollards, the followers of Wycliff. It was he who fulfilled his promise to the Papacy by his sanction of the first English law for the burning of heretics. The victory on the field of Bosworth, in 1485, won chiefly by the strategy of the Stanley, had dethroned Richard III. and taken his life, had made the Earl of Richmond, with the fallen crown placed on his brow by Stanley, Henry VII., and had given the brave Stanley the rank of Earl of Derby. The marriage of this new Earl to the widowed mother of Henry VII. gave him relations to royalty, and a place in the centre of arbitrary Tudor ideas. The Wars of the Roses, ended by the marriage of Henry of Lancaster to Elizabeth of York, left the Earl high in the despotism of the time. The spirit of the Stanley policy in Man may be thus accounted for, and a comment be found in the counsels of father to son in 1643. In addition, there were habits of government under the English crown. In Ireland, one of the Earls, under the Tudor rule, had been Lieutenant for many years. The sympathy of "the great Earl" with the Stuart dynasty is historic, and was repaid with characteristic ingratitude. The long absences of the Earls in the great affairs of State, left the little Island to the tyranny of subordinates, one of whom, in 1588, the Earl had to reprimand for oppression which could no longer be endured. The strength of the Stanley position with royalty, even at a much earlier period than the era now named, was seen in the summary dismissal of the five ecclesiastical Barons who refused homage. Without the intention, the act made the transition from Popery much easier ages after.

At the same time, with this strong rule, it must be admitted that in the Stanley character there was a liberal churchmanship. An illustration occurs in the ordination of the great John Howe, in the church at Winwick, not far from Knowsley, and one of the rich Derby livings. The ordainers were the Rector and his curates, all Presbyters, and no Bishop. The event would hardly have taken place, almost under the eye of the patron, had he been a High Churchman. It was an anticipation of the action of Wesley in his ordinations to the ministry for the United Kingdom and the United States, holding, as the New Testament shows, that Bishop and Presbyter are of the same order in the Christian ministry. But to return.

As honour and as property, the Island would have but a secondary place amid the distinctions and possessions of the House of Derby. The earl refused the ancient title of king, preferring, as he said, to be a great peer rather than a petty king, and the Island was not likely to command much attention from him and his. They had their place, as has been already noted, amid the great affairs of English history, some in the first rank of statesmanship, of government, and of war. Immense English wealth came with honour, in the marriage of Sir John Stanley with the heiress of Lathom ; with multiplied gifts of land from royalty ; with the Barony of Strange ; from Henry VIII., and Edward VI., and Mary ; previously, from Henry VI., for services in Wales ; from Elizabeth, for six years' government as Lord Deputy in Ireland; from Edward IV., for warlike services against the Scots ; and from Richard III. Much wealth in Lancashire and Cheshire thus came to the Stanleys. In the whole there was great personal distinction. In addition to the fame of Bosworth and of other scenes of war, the Stanley history records the conspicuous part taken by Sir John Stanley in the Battle of Poictiers in 1357, and in the Battle of Shrewsbury in 1403, against the Earl of Northumberland, with Henry IV. The Stanleys lived in the first style of the English peerage. The burial of the Earl in 1572 was with almost royal state.

The position and wealth of the Stanley House will thus in part explain neglect of Manx interests. The Murrays of Athol formed a contrast. The Island was guarded as a source of wealth, and hard bargains with the British Government brought them some hundreds of thousands of pounds.

It may be allowed to add that the favour of royalty seems to have left the seventh Earl, who, notwithstanding his great services to the Stuarts, was treated by them with cold suspicion and ingratitude, the Earl at last losing life and estates in the tragic execution at Bolton in 1651. It is curious to note, collaterally, that another Stanley, not in the direct line of heirship, Sir Edward Stanley, was made Lord Monteagle by Henry VIII. for his services in the battle of Flodden Field, in 1573. Through his grandson came the letter that saved James I. and his Parliament from the Gunpowder Plot; the same was great grandson of the Thomas Stanley, who was once Bishop and Governor of Man.

Among the hindrances to Manx freedom must be ranked the influence of Romanism on the Government. Its power was great in the earlier ages. The priestly jurisdiction was independent of the civil. The lord of the Isle might not intrude within the barriers in affairs civil or criminal, and of course not in affairs ecclesiastical. The Bishop had his court, his officials, and his prison, and also his place in the legislature. In the canon law, the ecclesiastical courts, the penal power; from the Norwegian Archbishop of Drontheim, from Furness Abbey, and the Priories external to the Island, and from the Pope of Rome, and yet later from Canterbury and York, came thus the restraint on Manx liberty. The Canon law, at three separate Synods from 1239 to 1350, and numbering fifty-three Canons, was supreme in the Diocese, and controlled Manx life personal and social. The octopus had completely enwrapped its prey. The position of Manx freedom may be imagined from what we know of modern Popish countries, Ireland included. The character of the priesthood is seen in some of the episcopal prohibitions as to frequenting or keeping public-houses. There are no traditions of religious zeal such as have come from Iona, Lindisfarne, and Whithorne; no evidences of the use of the Manx language, rather than the Latin of the Romish service, for worship and instruction. The Latin service was the rule in England until 1517. The monks of Rushen wrote their history in Latin. Nothing sacred is left in early Manx. The result in popular ignorance and in morals, as well as in the true freedom of man, all increased by isolation, may be inferred.

Celtic Christianity had been of a purer type in the ages of Ninian, St. Patrick, and Columba, and on to 560 and beyond. The intimate relations of Man to the outer ecclesiastical bodies, may have at first sprung from the purer ages of faith. Organised Romanism, as we have seen, had no place in these kingdoms before 597, when Augustine came from Rome. The resistance of the British Churches to his mission is historic. Not until 664 did England yield to the Papal claims, nor Ireland, which had closer relations to Man, until 1164. The first Romish Bishop in Man must have been long after the time of Augustine, and centuries after the age of St. Patrick. It was about 595 that the Priory of Bangor sent Columbanus on his great European mission, just before the attack of Rome on British Christianity. The ages of corruption came quickly on, as seen around the great monasteries of Wearmouth, Ripon, and Furness, to mention no others; relics, the added Sacraments, the assertion of superhuman power in the priesthood, all the essential elements of the Papal system gained ascendency. The Isle of Man would share in this tendency, with its loss of truth and liberty. The midnight of the darkness was 1219, when the Island became a fief of Rome. The Manx Monastery became an organic part of the Romish system, so that in 1044, at the Synod of London, one of the monks of Rushen became Abbot of Evesham. The restraint on Manx freedom remained long after 1537, when Henry VIII. claimed the resources of Rushen Abbey.

The course of *legislation* did not much help the interests of the people. It was more to the advantage and power of the Lord of the Isle. For many ages, there had been no trial by jury; sheep stealing, and even petty dishonesty were made liable to capital punishment. It was felony to leave the Island without permission from the government. The authorities claimed labour at reduced wages, arbitrarily fixed. At last came the crowning injustice in the change of the tenure of the land, turning freehold into leasehold, with three lives, and, in effect, making men tenants of what had been their own. It was a revival, in 1643, by the Earl of Derby, of the injustice of Godred Crovan in the eleventh century, after the battle of Sky Hill; the result was a feeling of rebellion which compelled the Earl to hasten to the Island, and which was suppressed by measures of crafty policy mingled with secret arrangements for defence. After holding two courts of Tynwald, he found a basis for peace with the people, and thus ended the threatening commotion.

With unjust laws, there was an administration uncertain in its justice. From 1533 to 1569, eight of the Governors were of the Stanley family, and several after that time. A self-elect House of Keys was subordinate to the ruling power, which had no liking for popular rights. The administration seems to have disposed the people to accept the rule of the Commonwealth, and to refuse hopeless resistance in the interest of the Earl. Just as the action of 1643 was the consummation and evidence of unjust legislation, the treatment of William Christian, the "Iliam Dhone" of Manx history, who was executed at Hango Hill in 1662, under the charge of treason to the Earl, was the supreme evidence of unjust administration long continued. The history is a long one, and has been much debated, but we may give a summary of the ruling facts: The alleged treason was the surrender of the Island, in 1651, to the Parliamentary forces in Ramsey Bay. Christian was Receiver-General, and had the insular forces under his command. In judging of the final sentence, it is not necessary to assume that Christian was faultless. It may be admitted that in 1658 his administration of insular funds had not been honest, and that two opinions might be held of the surrender, that of the Countess of Derby at Castletown, negotiating for the life of the Earl, then a prisoner of war in Chester Castle, and urging resistance to the utmost by force; and that of Christian, with leading men of the Island, who were left alone to contend with the ten ships of war with a fleet of forty-four other vessels, having on board military forces to compel surrender. There was no treason; the Earl was not king; the submission was to the power supreme in the United Kingdom at the time. The case between the imprisoned Earl and the Parliamentary power was entirely independent of the action of Christian at Ramsey. The execution of the Earl at Bolton, was for having fought against Parliament at Wigan and at Worcester in the interest of the Stuarts. At Ramsey, resistance meant useless bloodshed, and the Governor, Musgrave, choosing to remain away at Castletown, a responsibility fell upon Christian which did not entirely belong to his position. The Earl, by his action eight years previously as to the land, seems to have lost the affection of the Manx people, who now, indeed, were helpless before the Parliamentary forces. The surrender was not by Christian alone; with him were members of the legislature and chief persons of the Island. Perhaps they feared the sacrifice by the Derby family at Castletown of Manx rights in the peculiar circumstances of the Earl as a prisoner of war. Christian, after the Island hab deen handed to Lord Fairfax, and placed under Chaloner as Governor, was treated by the House of Stanley as if the past was blameless as to treason or any thing of the kind. Nine years after the submission to the Parliamentary forces, the name of Christian appears as a witness in the Commission issued by Earl Charles to settle some ecclesiastical affairs in the Island. By the Commonwealth Christian was made Receiver-General. In the Journal of the House of Commons under date of December, 1651, two months after the execution of the Earl at Bolton, and, of course, subsequent to the decisive scene at Ramsey, Christian is named as "an able and honest man" worthy of being consulted in the crisis. After an interval of eleven years or so the new Earl and his mother take action against Christian for his yielding to the forces of the Commonwealth in 1651. In 1660, that is, two years before these proceedings of vengeance for the past, there had been a general Act of Indemnity by Charles II. on his restoration to the throne, and when the Island was given back to the Stanleys, covering all political offences from 1637 to 1660. This, of course, included 1651. The insular judicial proceedings on the case, dictated by the Earl, were illegal, and in defiance of the King in Council, by which Court the case had been adjudged in 1662. Imperial orders had been sent to the insular authorities that the case brought by the Earl against Christian did not belong to insular jurisdiction, and that Christian must be given up to the English power. Trusting to the King's Act of Indemnity, he had ventured to return to the Island in 1662, and was then seized and imprisoned. Seven members of the House of Keys, on their refusal to take part in the trial, were arbitrarily dismissed by the Earl from their places in the legislature and replaced by seven others more pliable. For refusing the concurrence in the sentence of death, one of the Deemsters was also deposed and another substituted. Meanwhile, the action taken in the Island was disallowed by the King in Council, the appeal of Christian for protection under the Act of Indemnity allowed, and Earl Charles ordered to send Christian to London to be heard by the supreme authority. The royal order from the English Government was concealed by the Governor, and the proceedings hurried on, with the result of the immediate execution of Christian at Hango Hill. The judicial sentence from England immediately followed, holding that the blood of Christian had been shed unjustly, commanding the Governor and Deemsters to appear before the King in Council, requiring them to pay the costs of the prosecution, the two Deemsters to be imprisoned for further proceedings, the Governor reprimanded for keeping secret the royal order to suspend the sentence of death to give time for further consideration, the deposed Deemster to be restored to his office, and the estates and other property of Christian to be given back to his widow and family. The action of the Earl Charles was in the old spirit of the Stanley administration, but in this instance stained by blood shed unjustly. In that seventeenth century, Manx rights were but slightly regarded.

Thus far for civil freedom. Let us turn to religious liberty. The appointment of Bishops as Governors—"sword bishops" as they were termed—was a hindrance to religious liberty. The powers of the Bishop had around them the prestige and terrors of the civil authority. The *Ecclesiastical*

Constitutions of Bishop Wilson, enacted at the time of the Act of Settlement in 1703, though without the "sword," were a sufficient terror to the Nonconformist conscience. It placed the Manx people under the Canon law with its searching powers over religious convictions, and family and social life. For conduct implying no violation of civil law—not attending church, not observing church forms, it had its penance and its prison enforced by the civil power, under the orders of the Bishop's Court, and without appeal to the law of the land. Persons could thus be fined, sent from parish to parish in the white sheet of penance, and in the public market, thrown into prison, dragged through the sea at the tail of a boat manned by the Governor's authority, outlawed to a great degree, and "left severely alone." None neglecting confirmation could be married. In the absence of other evidence on religious matters, the individual could be questioned on oath for self-accusation. Poor Kate Kinrade was dragged through the sea in Peel Bay; the Clerk of the Rolls was sentenced to prison by the Bishop, who refused even the right of self-defence under the charge. At last the case of Mary Henricks made the cup overflow so as to call forth the Earl of Derby himself to interfere, and reverse the Bishop's sentence. In the final issue came the conflict between the Church Courts and the civil government, the closing scenes being Bishop and his two Vicars-General being thrown into the prison at Castle Rushen, by the authority of the Governor; though, on appeal to the English Government, the action of the Governor was not sustained. It is not surprising that, amid modern enlightenment, these "*Constitutions*" should have become obsolete; though one wonders that they should still have a place in the laws of the Manx people. The boast that there were no Manx Nonconformists in those days—as the case of the persecuted Manx Quakers proves—was explained by the rigour by which Canon law denied the rights of conscience. On the whole, then, during the 330 years of Stanley ascendency, from 1406 to 1736, when the Murrays of Athol succeeded, with no advantage, to freedom, the advance in liberty was but slight. During the interval the House of Keys had been seldom convened.

Manx Freedom: The Progress.

CHAPTER IX.

MANX FREEDOM: THE PROGRESS.

FROM the descent of the ages, towards the loss of freedom, let us turn to consider the sources of the liberties now enjoyed.

From and after the earlier years of the sixteenth century the spirit of the time favoured progress in freedom. The nations of Europe had become weary of oppression, and the energies of the Lutheran age were aroused. The tendency was strong towards political change, for the advantage of the people. The influences of the great movement could not but reach Man.

The early abolition of Popish Institutions in the Island (1422) had been of unlooked-for advantage to the later reformation. Papal supremacy and popular liberty cannot exist together. The suppression of the ecclesiastical Baronies, with their separate jurisdictions, had been a large contribution towards Manx freedom. Only the Bishop remained, with the semblance of a Baron, but bound to hold the stirrup of the Stanley as he mounted into the saddle at the close of the annual meeting of Tynwald. The question of priestly supremacy was finally settled in relation to the civil power. It was part of the Derby policy, and had much to do with Manx liberty. At times, indeed, it seemed uncertain. In 1505, the earl consolidated and confirmed to the Papacy various gifts and grants, following the course of his predecessor. There were close Romanist relations, for to the Earl's father, Cardinal Wolsey had been guardian and trustee. The Abbot of Rushen had been made Governor. The early Stanleys were Papists. The first Earl, he of Bosworth field, left £20 yearly to the convent near Lathom, for masses for his soul and for the souls of his relatives. One of the Stanleys became Bishop of Ely in Papal times, and died in 1525. He left directions that his tomb must bear the request for prayers for his soul. Still, the Stanley rulers would allow no priestly dictation in civil affairs : they were kings in Man. On August 22nd, 1422, when Sir John Stanley ended the independent jurisdiction of the Church Barons, and the right of asylum from the general law, he held his Court within the Bishop's ground, at Kk. Michael, thus visibly setting aside the ancient episcopal jurisdiction in civil affairs. There was rebellion ending in a riot in the churchyard, in resistance to the action of the lord of the Isle, but the riot was put down with a strong hand, and the rioters adjudged liable to death. In the time of Wycliff, there were signs of sympathy with the Reformer, of political restraint on the system of Manx Popery, and Canon law was suppressed. The Barony of St. Trinion's which had belonged to the Prior of Whithorne, was forfeited to the lord of the Isle ; the church of St. Trinion's, begun when Scotland ruled, was never finished ; and the Derby power was the real "phynnodderee" which prevented the completion of the roof of the "Keill brish," now the interesting ruin which has a Sergeant appointed to its Barony from year to year.

In addition to the direct policy of the house of Derby, Canon law also lost its power, though in the energetic hands of Bishop Wilson, at a much later date than that just implied : it failed as a moral restraint, or social help to goodness, and in the end left him in disappointment and depression after an episcopate of fifty-eight years, extending from 1692 to 1750. Its failure as an obsolete weapon of the Papacy was the removal of another hindrance to the march of freedom.

There were, at the same time, special causes which made for freedom.

One was the general ownership of the land by the Manx people under the Act of 1703. The Island was a region of freehodls. There was no Squire of overshadowing ownership to control the popular liberties. There were forces in high places, when Manx Nonconformity, under the name of Methodism, began its course in 1775, which sought to destroy the new movement; but a site for a Methodist Chapel could always be secured from friends living on their own acres, and who were ready with cart and horses and money to help in building the house which bigotry hated. Among these freeholders were the Manx Methodists and Nonconformists, sheltered by their freeholds from oppression. Largely, these formed the constituencies of the Sheadings, to whom in 1866 came the rights of election, but who, in the time now referred to, had considerable social influence. The Institution of Tynwald was full of great possibilities, only needing development for freedom. The civil constitution had its House of Keys, Coroners for each Sheading, and their Deputies the Lockmen, the Moar to collect the lord's rent, the Sumner-General with his subordinates; and only the spirit of freedom was needed to transform the whole into what was worthy of Christian civilisation over a free people. Yet more complete were the methods adopted when, in 1777, high bailiffs were appointed to the towns, and who are now supplemented by Justices of the Peace. Measures of improved law were gradually adopted, long before modern developments. In 1429 was enacted a law for the better protection of life and property, and for the prevention of trial by combat; and, in the year following, for the restoration of the House of Keys. Measures were taken for relief from ecclesiastical exactions, and the strange law excluding Scotchmen from the Island was repealed. These steps led up to the Act of Settlement in 1703. An Act in 1736 abolished the powers of the spiritual Courts, which had been so full of terror. A better administration followed ; public officials were dismissed for misconduct in the affairs committed to them, and even a Bishop reprimanded for misappropriation of funds. One of the greatest benefits was the Revestment of 1765, which transferred the sovereignty of the Island to the British Crown. It ended a personal, and sometimes unjust rule : smuggling could now be dealt with, and the Imperial Exchequer protected. Laws of Bankruptcy, which the administration of the House of Athol was somehow slow to repeal, were now easily dealt with on their merits. With the change came also the fuller shelter of British power, as by Elliot and his ships of war in the sea fight off Jurby, seen, it is said, at once from the roof of Bishop's Court and the opposite shores of Galloway, when the French Thurot attempted invasion. It allowed the better influences of the Commonwealth to pervade the island, for Fairfax naturally favoured freedom, was tolerant of the English Church, though the Bishopric was suppressed, and gave the funds thus available partly to the poorer clergy, and partly to the free education of the four towns.

I am indebted to the recent volume of Governor Walpole for the summary I now record of the constitutional present in Man, as given in *The Land of Home Rule*. There is, indeed, nothing in the Manx Constitution that would meet the wishes of the Home Rulers of Ireland, as will be seen from the facts : the Imperial power limits the insular power of legislation, has supreme authority without local concurrence, imposes the customs duties, controls the normal expenditure, leaving to Tynwald only the disposal of any surplus revenue. There is no insular power to withhold supplies for the redress of grievances; the expenditure of the government can be increased without local consent; the Governor has a veto on all expenditure. The Governor has no Cabinet and no Premier; he is Chancellor of the Exchequer, Home Secretary, President of the Local Government Board, has command of the Police, and has the sole executive authority. The relations to the British Government are through the Home Secretary. Since 1866, the House of Keys has been on the basis of popular election. The system of Manx government generally works without friction, and with a loyalty to the throne unsurpassed. The Council, which is the second legislative chamber, and co-ordinate in legislation, is composed of eight members, chiefly legal functionaries and paid officials, all *ex officio* in their place in the Council, three of the eight—the Bishop, the Archdeacon, and the Vicar-General — representing the interests of the Established Church. In the review of the course of freedom, we see the Island released from the violence of the early ages, invested with the privileges of civil and religious freedom, and under a government worthily administered. There is a healthy public opinion, pervaded by sound moral and religious principles, and sustained by the influence of prosperous Christian churches, with their Sunday-schools and other organisations, and, beyond this, influential temperance societies. The moral attitude of the Manx people is true to good order socially, and worthily guards the highest interests of Christian civilisation, from Port Erin to the Point of Ayre.

On each July 5th, the annual day of Tynwald, at St. John's Hill, there is an instructive summary of Manx rule. There are forms more ancient than those of the British

House of Commons, in the proceedings of the day. The Scandinavian feature, found in Shetland also, remains—the open air parliament and the Court of Justice. On the historic Hill, seated in state, is the Governor, as representative of the British monarch, with the sword of State before him, as tradition speaks of King Orry in the days of old; on the rising circular steps of earth are scattered the traditional rushes. The procession of the insular authorities has come to that central mound from the adjacent Church of St. John's—the Keys, the Council, the officials of the seventeen parishes, the Coroners, the Bishop, significantly alone, and, in the position of supremacy, the Governor. In attendance, gracing the procession, are the clergy of the Established Church; in the outer circle are the police, and beyond are the crowd, residents and visitors. Within a short distance is the railway for north and south, and near rises Slieu Whallyn, opposite the main mountain range. All being in order, there is next the formal promulgation of the laws of the past year, by the Coroner of Glenfaba, in both Manx and English, after which the procession re-forms and returns to the church, where the Tynwald Court completes the legal business of the day; and soon the Governor takes his departure, and the crowds disperse to their homes. The whole scene is half judicial, half poetic; but it shows the relations in Ellan Vannin of governor and governed. However designated, by the title of Home Rule or any other phrase, and however ample the space for further adaptations, it is a system in which Manx energy and moderation are at the oars, and English skill and tact at the helm, with a fair promise for the future course.

Many Wealth: Hindrances.

THOLT-E-WILL BRIDGE.

CHAPTER X.

MANX WEALTH : HINDRANCES.

N the discussion of Manx wealth, the term must be taken with moderation. There is no scope, either in the heirship of land, or the opportunities of business, for the accumulations of the millionaire. Conspicuous wealth is an exception; general competency and safe advance a characteristic feature.

In the history of the general subject may be noted some chief hindrances, in the early violence of invaders, in natural disadvantages, in the exactions of Romanism, and in the demands of the lords of the Isle.

1. The *invasions* and plunder of the early ages might well find expression in the Manx proverb, "Boght, boght dy bragh," "Poor, poor for ever." They came with irresistible force. They were part of the movement of the northern nations which affected other countries besides Man The Danes had found their way to the eastern coast of England, about 868, from Northumbria down to East Anglia. In the issue they conquered England, and for twenty-seven years, from 1017, held its sceptre, and extended their ravages to Normandy also. On the western side of England, the Norwegians came into the Irish sea, plundering the island and other places on their way from the north. From 91·2 to 1,065 seems to have been an interval of savage spoil. It is stated in some of the records extant, that Man was nearly depopulated by Harold of Norway, in 888, and that it was afterwards laid waste by Sweyn, his son. In 1077 came the

successful invasion of Godred Crovan, after two previous attempts, with his command of the island and seizure of its resources. He had escaped, as stated, from the Norwegian defeat at Stamford Bridge, near York, in 1066, by the English king, who himself the same year fell at the battle of Hastings before the Norman Conqueror. There were other conflicts added to those from without; a battle between north and south at Jurby, in 1098, the north victorious; another at Ramsey, in 1142, between Godred, son of Olave, and his nephew Reginald, the former slain, but avenged with terrible reprisals. Beween 1158 and 1164, arose the war which separated "Man" from "the Isles," Somerled taking the latter, but also plundering the Manx people. After an invasion with great slaughter, in 1182, came another in 1204, when John of England, in his invasion of Ireland, would not spare the little island. A little before this Reginald, dethroned, had laid waste the south. At other dates came marauders from Scotland, calling at Derbyhaven and Ronaldsway, and from Ireland. In 1228 occurred the battle between Olave and Reginald, at Tynwald Hill, when the latter lost his life. In the conflict at Ronaldsway was defeated Ivar, who had seized the throne on the death of Magnus, the last of the Norwegian line. Norway had sold "Man and the Isles" to Scotland for a capital sum and a yearly rent. Then occurred a succession of transfers which could have tended only to poverty; claimed by Edward I., given to Alfrica, sister of Magnus, and who had married Montacute, by whom the island was mortgaged to Beck, the opulent Bishop of Durham; after this given to other royal favourites. Still there were invasions: by the Scots, at Ramsey, in 1313, and at Castle Rushen; by the Irish, and by the French, all in quick succession. It would, under these circumstances, be with the Manx people, as previously with their Celtic kindred in Wales, Cornwall, and Cumberland, under the Saxon invaders—poverty and distress.

2. There were also *natural* hindrances to escape from poverty. In the isolation of the early times there could be but little commerce. Add to this the barren soil, the absence of manufactures, and the unskilled farming of those ages. There was no commerce to carry off the abundant fisheries of herring, cod, turbot, and shell fish. The cattle and produce of the farmer must remain without export; the mineral wealth was but slightly opened, though the resources of Laxey and Foxdale, as well as the quarries of lime and poolvash marble, could not be entirely unknown. There were no visitors as now. The time was far in the future when Ellan Vannin would become one of the chief watering places of the United Kingdom. The local demand for produce would, therefore, be small from farmer, shopkeeper, or merchant. There was no impulse to new houses in the building trade, nothing to give increased value to land. The smuggling which prevailed until the Revestment in 1765, would really bring no relief in its profits, and only demoralisation to the social condition. The lord of the Isle was supposed to derive some advantages when so slow to take legal steps in resistance, though the Imperial Exchequer had immense losses yearly by the want of restraint. The impulse also which came from the dishonest law of bankruptcy brought profit to a class, but was no source of real prosperity to the island.

3. The earnings of the working classes were low. As late as 1609, the year's wage of a ploughman, with board and lodging, was only 13s. 4d.; under the same conditions the mason and the tailor had but 4d. per day. The labourers were badly housed; coals, being imported, were too costly for their fires, and, in the towns, turf was not always within reach. The farmer had only low prices for his produce in

the market. In 1798, the prices were: for pork, 2½d. per pound; for ham, 5d.; for a couple of chickens, 6d.; for fowls, 12d. each (the shilling was 14d.); for geese, 1s. each. Crops, cattle, poultry, the dairy, the orchard, had no outlet beyond the Manx shores. The style of home life was humble: breakfast, porridge and milk; dinner, mainly potatoes and herring; supper, cowry or broash ; meat seldom, except on Sunday, when the savoury broth, thick with vegetables and enriched with the meat and pudding boiled in it, with barley bread, was a chief luxury; tea was deemed an extravagance leading to bankruptcy; occasionally there was a substantial meal of "Solaghan." In clothing, much was home-spun and home-woven; the children, often barefoot, the men behind plough and harrows, or in the field of green crops, wearing "carranes" for shoes. On the social level next above, of course, life had more luxury, though drapers' shops were few, even in the early years of the nineteenth century, the demands on the butcher limited, and no need of the poulterer's shop in Douglas itself.

The working classes were held down by the want of opportunity for education.

In the old time schools were few, and, with a few exceptions, feeble; the parish school especially. In those of the parish many of the children went barefoot. Each would daily take to the school a turf for the school fire, in the cold of winter. The masters and mistresses were often personally infirm, and humble in teaching ability; in my own list of schools, two were lame, one humpbacked, with a squint, another with a wooden leg. It is only just to add that in the succession were some of no ordinary qualifications. It must be admitted that in those days parental feeling was not awake to the value of an education more than commercial. This was no less true of the respectable farmer than of other classes. The results were what should have been foreseen. The prizes of civil life fell to strangers of better education. In some cases Manxmen held their own, particularly the Deemster's office, which required knowledge of the Manx tongue in Court, and others also did honour to their country by superior powers. Yet often, at the Bar and elsewhere, the Manxman had the disadvantage. The experience of English life and training won the forensic honours of years gone by for men like Roper, Dumbell, Bluett, and others who might be named. At other times, it is true, the promotion of strangers came from the patronage of the Stanleys and the Murrays, the last above all. The lesson of the whole, however, was the importance of the highest education, and of experience in cultured life. Where the opportunities were given, the gifts were found in science and philosophy, in the region of law, or in the greater affairs of imperial administration. It would be only just to apply to the Island the policy carried out in Ireland, Scotland, and Wales, and to award the best positions in public appointments—other things being equal—to men of the native race. This wise policy has been adopted in the recent appointment of Archdeacon, as in some past instances in other spheres.

4. Conspicuous among the hindrances to wealth must be named the exactions of Popery which drained the resources of the Manx people. The property and revenue of insular Popery, apart from the Establishments abroad, whose heads were at one time Barons of the Isle, were very considerable. The current demands for tithes and fees for the priesthood were only a part. Extensive lands were given to Bishop's Court, to Peel Cathedral, to Rushen Abbey, to the Nunnery, and to St. Trinion's. In 1219 the Island had been surrendered to the Pope, and placed under the obligation of a yearly payment. To the Bishop had been given, in addition to the lands just named, the Islet and

harbour of Peel, the revenue of the fishery there and in the Lake of Mirescoge, in Lezayre, with a margin of valuable property adjacent, and the tithes of the lead and iron mines, one penny for every house with a fireplace, an extensive turbary in the mountains, the Earl of Derby adding, in 1505, one-third of the manor of Kirby. The stretch of land between the Laxey River and the Dhoon Glen, and reaching from the sea to the mountains, was Church property. Rushen Abbey had, immediately around the Abbey, 422 acres of land, with cottages and mills, with 2,000 acres elsewhere, and with the right of fishing at Lezayre. The Nunnery had the tithes of many hundreds of quarterlands. As a survival, there are still "Sergeants" of lands in German, Lezayre, Lonan, Braddan, Malew, and Rushen. The Seneschal, Ecclesiastical Judge, the Sumner, the Vicars-General, were officials in Church affairs. The names of the Abbey lands in Lonan and Onchan, and of Ballamenagh—"the monks' farm"—still remain. The tithes and fees to the priests were enforced by the ecclesiastical Courts with the terrors of Canon law, extending from the money fine to excommunication and purgatory. On the list of priestly claims were the cattle of the farm, the pigs and poultry of the farmyard, the fish of stream and lake, every catch of herrings ; and, on land, the crops at harvest, the grain at the mill, the beer at the brewing, and a tax on each public-house and the products of the dairy. Three times a year there were oblations, and also fees for every stage of birth, marriage, death, for examinations in the faith, for acts of Church discipline, for masses for the dead. Intestate property came under priestly administration ; wills must be written by the priests.

The baronies external to the island had much in landed possession and in tithes. Rushen Abbey had been given to Furness Abbey, by Olave, in the twelfth century, and therewith the control of the Bishopric, one hundred quarterlands, and one-third of the insular tithes. Extensive properties with names not now understood, but sounding like Norwegian, were confirmed to Furness, by Pope Eugenius III., to which, in 1245, Harold made additions, including the mines of the Island, the "rectories" (so termed) of Michael and Maughold, three acres of land at "Bakewaldswath," and a meadow near St. Trinion's, named in Manx the "Lheannee runt," "the round meadow." To the Priory of Whithorne belonged five quarterlands and the Barony of St. Trinion's. "Bangor" was a general term in Welsh usage, meaning a college or monastery of distinction, and has been given to places in Flintshire, in Anglesey, and St. Asaph, as well as in Ireland (Bright). To the Bangor in Ireland, near Belfast, belonged eighty-six quarterlands in various parishes, and six which it held jointly with Sabal; to the Priory of Sabal—clearly distinct from Bangor, though in the same neighbourhood—was allotted a position showing that it had a share in Manx endowment, though with the exception of the six quarterlands mentioned, there does not seem to be any other property given in its list of endowments. The meaning of the term Sabal is somewhat difficult of definition, and suggests what is curious in Irish history. It is said that St. Patrick, in his last years, spent much of his time in Armagh, where, at a place named "Sabhal Pheric," understood to mean "Patrick's Barn," he established the Metropolitan See, where, it is alleged, he preached his first sermon in Ireland, and where he died in 465. A writer in *The Wesleyan Methodist Magazine*, of March, 1891, relates that the royal chieftain, Dicha, who dwelt on the south of the Strangford Lough, and had been converted under St. Patrick's ministry, made one of his barns into a place of worship, and that, on the same site, was afterwards built the famous church called, "Sabhal-

Padh:ig," rendered "Patrick's Barn." I am unable to say whether the term in Irish has the meaning supposed. To St. Bees belonged property in Groudle, in Maughold, and other places, the gift of Guthred, or Godred, and Reginald, lands extending from the Dhoon to Corna.

All these gifts and payments to the Papacy were, collectively, a large deduction from the temporal resources of the Island.

Largely, or entirely, the forfeited properties of the Barons were divided, it is said, between the Bishop and the poorer clergy.

5. The demands of the lords of the Isle in their administration were too heavy to be omitted from this category of hindrances to wealth. The lord of the Isle—Stanley or Murray—demanded yearly for his household, and his garrisons at Castletown and Peel, 500 beeves and a fixed supply of corn, and also a supply of turf and ling, without cost. Articles for his own use, otherwise subject to duty, were free to him, as also to the Bishop and Archdeacon. He claimed taxation on imports, and a part of all imported timber. Every season each fishing-boat had to pay him a contribution. By his authority were fixed the duties on imports and exports. The lord's rent was his, and one-fifth of the herring fishery. The officials of the Government, Clerk of the Rolls, and others, were not paid generally from revenue, but from their official fees, of which the lord, nevertheless, claimed a share. Out of the revenue the Deemster received only £13 6s. 8d. yearly. Under the oppressive exactions of the Government the net amount of the annual revenue fell to about £1,000, and the revenue was farmed for that sum to a Liverpool merchant. The Bishopric was sometimes vacant for an interval of years—once for seventeen years—and the moneys thus accruing did not appear to the credit of any public department. At last the lord claimed

the land as his own, and the people as his tenants. This was the Stanley of 1643, but the Murray who followed, in 1736, was equally grasping of insular resources. The clergy narrowly escaped the loss of Bishop Barrow's benefaction, who, at the cost of £1,000, had bought for the poorer clergy a portion of the tithes belonging to the Earl of Derby. For a time the Deed could not be found; the Duke of Athol claimed the tithes, and was hindered from the appropriation only by the son of Bishop Wilson accidentally finding the Deed, after anxious search.

During the Athol rule, from 1736 to 1830, some laws were passed which, with whatever advantage to the Duke, brought demoralisation to the people. Such was the law of bankruptcy which held its sway from 1737 to 1814; such was the lax administration towards smuggling which at last led the Imperial Government to seek the Act of Revestment as a defence of the Exchequer, the loss to which was valued at £350,000 each year. Against the will of the Keys and the people, negotiations were urged on with the English Government, for the sale of the Duke's rights and privileges which brought him £70,000, an annuity of £2,000, then £3,000 more for insular revenue, and, as lord of the manor, £416,114. For his interest in the Abbey lands, and in the forfeited properties of Bangor, Sabal, St. Trinion's, and Bishop's Court, he obtained a further sum. To give the Duke's nephew time to reach the canonical age the Bishopric was left vacant for several years after the decease of Bishop Cregan, in 1814. The tithes of the green crops which had ceased from the episcopate of Bishop Wilson, the new Bishop attempted to revive, but the attempt was abandoned from fear of the popular indignation. In compensation for payments to the Duke for his rights, the English Government now claims out of the Manx revenue the yearly sum of £10,000.

Manx Wealth: Helps and Sources.

RAMSEY.

CHAPTER XI.

MANX WEALTH: HELPS AND SOURCES.

THERE are many helps to material prosperity, notwithstanding the early adversity of the Manx people.

1. At the foundation of this statement are the industrial qualities of the Manx character. To begin with, there is superiority to the spirit of pauperism. There is often an unwillingness to accept of charity. I have known the labourer of lowly position provide for old age out of his savings. The principle appears on the broader scale of the community. There is no appeal to Government for help to build the railway, or to provide fishing boats and tackling. For such there is local capital. The noble fleet of fishing boats connected with Peel, and engaged chiefly on the coast of Ireland, the large fleet belonging to the herring fishery around the island, the smaller efforts of the humbler craft, are all of unaided ownership. There is a correlative kindness to the poor, which is another Manx feature. For many ages the poor were supported by voluntary provision; the beggar was helped by relief in kind, if not in cash, and in the country sometimes found the farmhouse with the bed specially arranged for such as he, and with supper and breakfast besides. In other cases, poverty was relieved by relatives. Subscriptions and public collections were readily given, and the kind legacy was frequent. Of this free tendency the House of Industry, in Douglas, and almshouses there and

in other parts of the Island stand in evidence. The gift of the hospital by Mr. Noble, though not a native, is of the same character. The modern refusal of voluntary subscriptions for the poor by many in Douglas and Ramsey has led, in those towns, to a levying of a poor rate, a costly alternative which the other sections of the island have avoided by the old method which provided as well or better for the poor. The mentally afflicted were cared for on the voluntary method, mostly by the charity of kindred or others; while now the asylum rate is required. The following are the statistics of pauperism and of the asylum near Douglas.

1. Statistics of Pauperism: The Government Return for 1893 reports an outlay of £2,606 for Douglas, and for Ramsey £622. In many of the parishes the rate-in-aid is not in operation; they are not bound to give any returns, and do so very reluctantly. The Island, for the most part, adheres to the old system of voluntary relief.

2. Statistics of the Lunatic Asylum: The number of patients is not given in the Returns: it is probably about 200 in the Douglas Asylum; the cost for 1893 was £5,261. For the Ramsey Poor Asylum, the outlay was £319. The numbers and cost seem exceptionally large in proportion to population.

A great Manx feature is industry. It has prevailed notwithstanding the Manx proverb, "Boght, boght dy bragh," "poor, poor for ever." There is much to interest in the study of the old industrial life, before the age of machinery, and of wholesale establishments. Home wants were met chiefly by home manufacture. In agriculture, machinery had not lessened the demand for rural labour. The skilled labour of the man with a trade was often under the home roof: the weaver, the shoemaker, the tailor, except when he and his apprentices went to board at the farmhouse to give the men a new outfit for the year. The hatter's workshop was not distant from the house, nor the joiner's; the blacksmith not usually far away, but at the meeting place of three or four roads central to a neighbourhood; the millwright would perhaps be the joiner, under a new form of his genius, for the threshing and winnowing machines needed by the farmer. Beyond these homely spheres would be the shipyard, with its occasional launch for home or foreign trade, or for the fisheries. The work of the farmhouse was mostly by wife and daughters, and included house, dairy, poultry, and the calves and pigs in their younger days. The kitchen "sided" for the evening, the wife would sit down to her spinning wheel, the hum mingling with the conversation which discussed the parish news. The quiet chair in the corner, near the fire with an open chimney for the turf smoke, would be occupied by the silent listener of the elder generation. In the season the female members of the household would take their place in the haymaking and the corn shearing, and would not be absent from the "Mheillea" at the end. In the summer, perhaps the sons would be off to the herring fishing; in winter, they would handle the flail and prepare for the corn merchant. With no butcher in the parish, the time would come for the killing of the fatted pig, taken as a scene emblematic of social commotion, in English, "the murdering of the pig and the cry of the geese." Once a year there was the family brewing, with sacks of barley in the "clay dub," the malting in the barn, with the stages following, not always to be commended. In the fine days of summer the annual turf digging would call away to the mountains. The licence monopoly, ending its year on each 30th June, and yielding to a limited class of merchants an "unearned increment" of much commercial value, had its great stir, then, of final imports in the harbours. Smuggling, too, was not forgotten. For a short interval the

Ball, at Kirby and elsewhere, would give an impulse to business. But industry was still the great feature of Manx life. Its style truly was primitive ; in Douglas, for example, no police, only one constable, with an assistant in emergencies ; no waterworks, only two water-carts, to help those who could not help themselves ; no gas-works, but the lamp lighter, with his torch and ladder ; no regular steamboat service but the smack, with possibly two days at sea, as I have known, between Whitehaven or Liverpool ; the carrier, three or four hours to Ramsey ; no post delivery but at the window. So life was isolated, business free from the modern worry, and general society leisurely; but things sanitary often neglected, and cholera left to reap its harvest.

The industrious life, though often busy, had its relaxations, as well as freedom from worry such as is common now. In the country, the farmers rose early, but the evenings of leisure were long. There was buoyancy in the merry hayfield, in the days of harvest, in the turf digging in the mountains. The Christmas "Oie'l verry," "the night of Mary," had in its "carval" singing more of the musical than of the religious. Often superstition relaxed into the humorous, in the transparent imposture of being carried off by the fairies, when people did not wish to be within reach at home, as I have known in the case of a bride who, having secured a husband, and the united passage being taken for America, followed her wish and was missing until the ship had sailed ; when she reappeared, saying she had been with "the fairies"; or the long moonlight evenings would be utilised by young men for the humorous, by startling an eccentric farmer, known to have his gun ready, the scarecrow placed within sight from the door, and, on the gun being fired, falling, pulled by one of the company behind the hedge, by means of a "sogaan," or straw-rope. Sometimes the relaxation, if less playful, was more rational, as in the practice of the singing class, or the experiments of the electrical machine. Simplicity and moderation in style of living, another Manx feature, are efficient aids to the temporal. Families living on their own acres, or other resources, are not ashamed to do the house work where servants might be employed. The "eirey" would follow the plough; the daughters would make a servant unnecessary; living plain, while substantial; dress in comely homeliness; the house of past generations sufficient; the family self-contained in its comfort; and, in past days especially, the yearly visit to somewhere unnecessary. Enterprise is not absent from these several business virtues. This appears in the home life, and yet more in the movements of emigration to other lands, though the Manxman is credited with caution excessive in its restraint. Caution is not a universal disadvantage; it holds back enterprise at times, but it also prevents rash speculation. Perhaps there is some excess of the quality in the Manx character. If so, it would not be unnatural; the Manx history is one of evil treatment for ages by foreign oppressors. Not seldom the stranger has come with an unknown history, taken advantage, and after being trusted has decamped into the unknown whence he had come. There was once an exclusive Manx law, giving a creditor the power of summary arrest, on seeing the stranger preparing for a passage over the sea. The same caution was suggested by frequent change in the ownership of the Island, and which, though not easily traced in their times and conditions, must have disturbed substantial interests treated thus with arbitrary disregard. With means generally limited, they could not afford to lose. The absence of provision in law for poverty, tended to prevent the speculative and adventurous. A modern feature is the formation of syndicates for the erection of large hotels and other structures, requiring a large capital with some uncertainty in the issue. The decisive money power in these does not come from Manxland, but from purses beyond the sea. Much of the house property for the accommodation of visitors and the resulting business belongs to English management and enterprise. It is all fair in trade and business. If caution withholds Manx people from such schemes, or want of capital, they must be content with the result, whether gain or loss. And one great advantage of the feature in its Manx measure, is the slowness in adopting untried measures which has refused rash innovations and left Ellan Vannin with a civil constitution whose roots go far deeper into the past than those of the British Constitution, and whose development has been without violent revolution. A policy is thus natural which makes legal changes reliable, if sometimes too slow, while it admits improvement and enterprise in all departments of the State. Emigration has been named as one form of enterprise. There are thousands of Manx people in the United Kingdom and the Colonies, and in the United States of America. Such congestion of the population as prevails in the Scotch Highlands and in Ireland has been thus prevented.

2. With the industrial qualities of the Manx character may be noted the commercial opportunities.

The restitution of 1703 for the injustice of 1643, the Act of Settlement, began an era of prosperity in the Island. The land had fallen out of cultivation, and it proved of as much advantage to the Earl of Derby as to the former tenants to restore to the people their rights. The value of the land has greatly increased under modern methods of cultivation. Rents were first enforced in 1505. Early ownership often appears in the name of the farm, as Ballagawne, Ballaquayle, Ballaradcliffe: the name in Manx may be taken to imply antiquity, as :

Lough ny yie . . . . . the lake of the goose.
Rhenbwee . . . . . the yellow division.
Rhenscault . . . . . the burnt division.

It is an exception to have English names. Some changes in the law had brought amelioration. The law of tithes was mitigated by commutation in 1839. The monopoly of a limited class of merchants and grocers and groups of private individuals, by a licence to import spirits, wine, tea and sugar, and other articles subject to duty—the quantity allowed to the Island each year being limited and fixed—had brought a considerable income to some, and to others reduced expenditure, but has been abolished. Land and commerce are on the same level. There are, also, some exemptions in taxation: there is no income tax or legacy duty ; no excise duty, except a small duty on beer ; and no poor rate, except, as already stated, at Douglas and Ramsey. The landed interest shares largely in the advantages accruing from the position of the Island as a resort for visitors ; the tenant farmer, or owner, has large receipts for poultry and garden produce in the season, and the value of land near the towns is greatly increased, while, indirectly, he shares in the general impulse to business.

The opportunities of trade and commerce are considerable. In addition to the business establishments, are the public companies, the mines, the fisheries, the shipping and commerce, and, above all, the visiting seasons yearly. The sphere of ambition, it will be admitted, is limited, compared to the broad English opportunities, for the professions or for commerce ; the man of genius, like Forbes in philosophy ; or of power in administration, like Cubbon in India, must not stay at home. Yet there are prizes within reach, and a good average of facilities for fortune. The old isolation is gone. The Island has become full of business energy, and a meeting place for the three kingdoms, with their hundreds of thousands seeking health and recreation. The towns, once fixed in outline, are extending; Douglas, at once towards Onchan along the coast, and inland towards the west; Ramsey, from its mountain background, enlarging north and west; Peel, Port Erin, Port St. Mary, and Laxey share the impulse. In the towns, Boards of Commissioners, with their municipal powers; in the House of Keys, self election at an end; in the administration, response to popular convictions; in the education of the people, the compulsory and the universal; everywhere, the energy of business; beyond, the flow of inrushing English life; the Manx language retiring before the Anglo-Saxon; the foreign element gaining social power. The social foundations are in course of being relaid. Freedom has new opportunities. The increase of substantial means has brought new powers of progress. Improved legislation has moved in the way to order and liberty. The stagnation of the eighteenth century has been followed by movements full of promise; it had its single lighthouse on the red pier in Douglas, but with no jetty to save from the rock opposite; no tower of refuge on Conister; no breakwater in the bay; no lighthouse on the Head, and no drive around it; no promenade along the shore; no electric tramway to Laxey. Now, all is the reverse, energy and commercial stir. In the country, agriculture has followed English improvements: for "carranes" there are shoes, and for the turf fire on the hearth, the "chiollagh," the "slowrie," and the open chimney, there is the better modern style. Habits, too, and social ideals, take a higher moral tone. Less litigation would still be an improvement, but movement is in the right direction; temperance has changed the character of the club anniversary, and of the Saturday at market. It would not now be necessary, as the late Mr. Bluett deemed it in his day, to defend the refusal of a challenge under the duel code by publishing a volume on the subject. The sacred ministries of truth have done much to transform the life of the Island. Smuggling has died out. Men of money power, hardly of a number to form a class, used to give cause to complaints of usury and oppression; but that day seems also to have passed. Among the Manx people now are the usual elements of English life: the culture, the School of Art, the Free Library, and such institutions, in aid of modern development.

The great foe to the success of industrial life, here, as elsewhere, is "the drink." The Temperance movement has done much to lessen the evil. Most of the Churches have their Temperance Societies and Bands of Hope, with others not so connected. The effect is seen in social reformation, as well as in public opinion and legislation. The "drunk and disorderly" show reduced figures. Yet the alcoholic position is strong: the duty on malt in 1893 was £2,221, and on imported liquor £39,067. Customs and license duties amount to above £44,000. The estimated outlay by visitors is £40,725; by the resident population, £121,151. Two-thirds of the crime come from "the drink." Unfortunately the law allows the visitors in their Sunday excursions to be *bonâ fide* travellers at the public-house.

Meanwhile, the insular wealth may be approximately seen in such facts as the following, for which I am in part indebted to Governor Walpole's recent volume, *The Land of Home Rule*, 1893.

The Insular revenue, £76,738; the Bank deposits . £1,670,684
The Insular expenditure 60,000
The gross annual value, including towns and parishes . 406,045

ELLAN VANNIN.

Government Grant towards popular education	£8,844
Expenditure under Local Commissioners	62,389
Receiving poor relief (out of a population of 55,608)	938
Rates for local expenditure	33.720
Estimated value of metal from the mines : various ores.	£7,727
The customs revenue (1892)	65,812
Agricultural rental value	100,000
The lord's rent (yearly)	1,500
The national debt	300,000

Taxation is lighter than in other parts of the kingdom. When given to Sir John Stanley in 1406, the annual value of the Island was £400; at the Revestment, it was about £7,293.

Social Changes: Transition from Romanism.

RUSHEN ABBEY.

CHAPTER XII.

SOCIAL CHANGES: TRANSITION FROM ROMANISM.

HE expression "Manx Reformation" does not often occur in Manx history; it is once used by Bishop Wilson where he states that it came later than the English Reformation. The full transition meant by the words has, however, taken place, for there was once a period of mediæval Papal darkness, and there is now an era of evangelical light.

The primary blow to Manx Popery was in 1422, when the ecclesiastical barons were disestablished and disendowed who refused their homage at Tynwald to the lord of the Isle, the rest submitting, and the civil authority made supreme over the ecclesiastical. Between 1521 and 1594, as the course of legislation shows, it is evident that the Derby rule was not unwilling to see changes both in doctrine and ritual. The annexation of the diocese to the province of York in 1542 favoured right tendencies; though it seems premature in Bishop Merrick, in 1577, to state that there was universal conformity to the formularies of the Church of England, while in 1594 it was still necessary to forbid prayers for the dead and other Popish practices. In 1660 mention is made of the Book of Common Prayer as part of the Church service and as enforced by a Commission appointed by the ruling Earl. An official letter from the Archbishop of York to Bishop Hildesley urged greater freedom from Popish observances, and public feeling began to demand further reformation. Yet the silent flow of events had been favourable. There was substantial release from Papal supremacy, and Romish practices were forbidden. The Prioress of the Nunnery had, in 1538, ventured on marriage. In 1569 a married clergyman (Salisbury) became Bishop. The restrictions on the marriage of the clergy were removed in 1610. In 1688 it was reported by the Bishop that the people were "nothing inclined to Popery," though the view was too sanguine, for several of the old Popish customs had been retained. Not until 1736 was the Spiritual Court abolished, with its fines, imprisonment, and excommunication. Religious liberty and the rights of conscience were denied until late in the Reformation movement; and the shadows of the old system lingered over clerical ministration. The great doctrine of the Lutheran Reformation—justification by faith in Christ—had not risen upon the island. But the movement gradually increased in power; steps were initiated for a Manx translation of the Scriptures; and in 1775 the Methodist revival gave to the Reformation its full development in the preaching of the Gospel. In the progress of things, a lectureship against Popery was endowed at St. George's Church, in Douglas.

There were reasons for this slowness in the Reformation. Manx Romanism does not seem to have been of an earnest type. There was no leader in the Reformation as in the method of Reformers elsewhere. There was not the conviction to produce martyrs, nor the hostility which the martyr spirit awakens. The tide slowly rose, without the storm, from 1422 to 1775. The Government policy caused delay. The Stanleys themselves had been Papists. To a great extent their collision with Romanism had been on political grounds. In the earlier days, in the days of Wycliff, there were signs of Stanley sympathy with the Reformer; and, later, as the third volume of the

Manx Society shows, there was continued antipapal legislation; yet policy sometimes restrained. In the interval of the Commonwealth, new impulses were given toward Reformation. Under Chaloner as Governor, from 1651 to 1660, it is true the Bishopric was suppressed; but there was much religious enthusiasm in the age, and the clergy were allowed to retain their livings, though the island had been transferred from the Earl of Derby to Lord Fairfax. And yet the onward movement fell short of completeness.

The transition from the old superstition had at first been but limited. For a time it was chiefly a protest against Papal supremacy and ownership, a withdrawal from the former ecclesiastical relations, a transfer of the headship of the Church from the Pope to the monarch, a change without the theology and spirit of the great Reformation; it was also a continuance of some essential errors, and of the denial of religious liberty to those who might not conform; it was largely the Anglican ideal, admired by Keble in his *Biography of Bishop Wilson*, which is substantially Popery under Canterbury instead of Rome. As initiated, it was not even doctrinal, still less evangelical. When two centuries had passed since the great Reformation, the Manx people were still without the Scriptures in the native tongue. There was no formal change in doctrine, after the manner of the English movement. The canons adopted at Braddan and elsewhere in the dark centuries remained and were, in substance, re-enacted in 1703. We note no adoption in form of the Thirty-nine Articles, and no revision of the terms of union with the State. It was the same Bishop, Thomas Stanley, one of the Derby family, at once Governor and Bishop, both before and after the English Reformation. He held the position from 1542 to 1545, under Henry VIII., again in the reign of Mary, and then from 1562 to 1569 in the reign of Elizabeth. The difference could not then be great between the past and the present. Happily, the great Earl did not resist the reforming tendency, nor his Countess, who, as the family historian relates, disliked the ways of Rome, as indeed was likely in a descendant from the noble race of the Huguenots.

In its aspects and mode, the Manx Reformation was a striking contrast to what obtained elsewhere. It was without violent commotion. Possibly the old superstitions had not gained a strong hold. There is no evidence, I believe, that the priests ministered in the language of the people. The ordinary Romish service was in Latin ; was thus in Ireland until 1551, and, therefore, probably in Man. The monks of Rushen wrote in the Latin of their age, and even in giving the boundaries of their Manx properties used terms more like Norwegian than Manx. A church not using the native language of a people will never win their enthusiasm. A preacher who thinks in one language and, mentally translating, speaks in another, can never mightily move what to him are a foreign community. The principle explains the failure of the Established Church in Ireland; the peculiar position of Methodism in the island where at first, when Manx was essential, the preaching was largely by native local preachers, to "the manner born," and accounts, perhaps, for the popular indifference when Man left its old profession.

The contrast between the quiet course of the Manx Reformation and the reformation in other lands where martyrs died is singular. The Lollards, under the rule of Henry IV., who gave the island to Sir John Stanley, were the victims of violent persecution. In the time of his successor, Henry V., Huss was martyred, and the bones of Wycliff burnt to ashes. In Ireland, in 1540, under Henry VIII., when Monarch displaced Pope, society was deeply stirred, though the change was remote and almost theoretical. In Mary's time the fires of Smithfield were kindled. A few years after came the massacre of the Huguenots, and then the Spanish Armada. In its reformation, Man was only slightly moved. Strange that in times when the principles implied moved Europe—the Waldenses, Flanders, Spain, Italy, and, near at hand, the Covenanters of Scotland—the Manx people did not share the commotion affecting religious life and freedom. That about the same time there should be much excitement because of the appropriation of tithes by the English Government, and, by the Lord of the Isle, of the one-third of the tithes which had belonged to Rushen Abbey, only shows how, under the Romish sway, the material eclipsed the moral in the Manx mind. It was a state of popular ignorance and insensibility which might partly come from the isolation of ages, but also from the moral prostration which the history explains. At last, however, the reforming movement, notwithstanding the peculiarities noted, reached its meridian, and the Manxman —like the labourer who looks at noon with shaded eyes to note the hour, and says "'Te vunlaa"—could say in a higher sense, "It is noon," and desire that the sun may no more go down.

ят Social Changes: The Established Church.

BISHOP'S COURT.

CHAPTER XIII.

SOCIAL CHANGES: THE ESTABLISHED CHURCH.

HE Manx Established Church is part of the Church of England, with the peculiarity of a petition in the Litany for "the blessings of the sea," as well as "the kindly fruits of the earth," with the sanction of the Legislature for its Canon law in Bishop Wilson's *Ecclesiastical Constitutions*, and the further fact, I believe, that it is not included in the Act of Uniformity. By Bishop Wilson it is termed a Protestant Church. In this chapter it is viewed from its beginning as a Church of the Reformation, though its previous conditions of origin will be within sight, and guidance must come chiefly from the volumes of the Manx Society.

Of the Manx Diocese no mention can be traced before 1098. It is said that there was a Bishopric of "Sodor," in 838, which included the Southern Hebrides, with Iona as centre; that the "Sodor Diocese" included the Islands of Bute and Islay, as well as Iona; that Man was anciently termed "one of the Sodor Islands"; that the twelve Franciscan Brethren at the Friary, in Arbory, are officially noted as within the Sodor Diocese; and that Man and the Sodor Diocese were thus united from 1098 to 1380, when the union ceased, the Manx no longer including the Hebrides, though retaining the "Sodor" as part of its title. A royal charter of the thirteenth or fourteenth century terms the Manx Bishop "the Bishop of Sodor." In the legal appointment of Bishop, care is taken to use the three phrases, "Bishop of the Isle of Man," "Bishop of Sodor," "Bishop of Sodor and Man." In the transfer of the Island from Norway to Scotland, in 1266, "Man" is distinguished from "the Sodors." The western islands of Scotland, north of Ardnamurchan, seem to have been termed "Nordereys"; those south of that point, "Sudereys." From 1098, for some time, the title was "Man and the Isles." The union with the State is from Norwegian arrangement.

The Manx Episcopate has been somewhat confused in its order from an attempt to claim great antiquity. The published list, which did not appear until the seventeenth century, is, in its earlier part, mere invention. It begins with Amphibalus, in 360. One of that name appears in the early history of the Church in Britain, and in his *Early English Church History*, Dr. Bright states that after the Dioclesian persecutions, a church in memory of him was built in Winchester, afterwards made into a cathedral, but no evidence exists of his being in Man; the list gives him eighty-four years as Bishop. St. Patrick follows in 444, of whose presence we have seen the lack of proof. To St. German some years are given, though it is historic that his sphere was Britain and Gaul, and that he died in Ravenna in 448. St. Maughold has given to him from 498 to 648, an episcopate of 150 years. To St. Conan and his three successors are given 241 years, 648 to 889, an average of sixty years. Yet the monks of Rushen had stated long before that nothing was known of Bishops in Man before the time of Godred Crovan (say 1077), and they insert the name of Roolwer as the first Bishop known to them, the last on their record being Duncan, in 1374. In the course of the history of the Bishopric there are intervals when there were no Bishops. In an early case the interval is forty years; under

THE ESTABLISHED CHURCH. 131

Elizabeth, three years; Charles I., seven years; the Commonwealth, nine years; from 1693, four years; from 1814, fourteen years. It is singular that with these facts Ward should assert in his *Ancient Records* that in the list of Manx Bishops the regular succession was never lost. In the *Annals of Ulster* for 798, published by Dr. Todd, mention is made of a " Dachonna, a Bishop of Man," but it gives no light to Manx history. With the exception of the nine years of the Commonwealth, there does not seem to be any account of the appropriation of the episcopal revenue during the vacancies. It appears that, until 1348, the Manx Bishops were generally consecrated at Drontheim, in Norway, whose Archbishop was Metropolitan. In that year Bishop Russell was consecrated by the Pope at Rome. Some of the Bishops were consecrated at Canterbury, some at York; some were appointed by Furness Abbey, others by Henry VIII., Mary, Elizabeth, and Charles II., and the lord of the Isle. One of the Bishops was Dean of Chester, as well as Bishop of Man, by the favour of Henry VIII., but without the concurrence of the Earl of Derby.

Until the last quarter of the eighteenth century (1775), the ministrations of the Manx Church included the whole population of the Island. It was said that there were no Nonconformists, but there were Manx Quakers in 1664, who were fined, imprisoned, and banished under the administration of Bishop Barrow, at once Governor and Bishop, while many were cast into prison also, as stated in Volume XI. of the *Books of the Manx Society*.

But little is known of the religious ministrations of the Manx clergy in the earlier days of the reformed Church. Among the clergy, the vicars had the prefix " Sir " to their name; the rectors were termed " Parsons." The livings generally were poor, often without a parsonage, or the parsonage in ruins. Some relief came in 1666 by the purchase of the impropriate tithes from the Earl of Derby by Bishop Barrow for £1,200, for the benefit of the poorer clergy. In the temporary loss of the Deed the endowment was nearly lost, being claimed by the Duke of Athol, but which was at last found by the son of Bishop Wilson among the documents of the C'erk of the Rolls.

As to the doctrines of the Manx Church from the time of the Reformation, the general position was that of Protestantism. It has been noted that Bishop Wilson termed it a Protestant Church. Whether there was a formal adoption of the Thirty-nine Articles of the English Church does not appear, so far as I have been able to ascertain ; they are not included in the Manx Book of Common Prayer, issued the year after its translation under the hand of the Bishop in 1761. Until 1772, after six years of learned toil, the Scriptures were given to the people in Manx. Prior to that date, only a few portions had been translated, and still fewer circulated, while of the 20,000 in the population more than two-thirds knew no language but their own. The Manx version is one of the great things achieved by the Manx Established Church. The work was committed to twenty-five Manx clergymen, who did their duty with adequate scholarship, translating from the original languages of Scripture, often in mutual consultation, and with the critical help, in special cases, of the two most eminent biblical scholars of the age, Bishop Lowth and Dr. Kennicott. Though the Manx translation has now passed out of popular use, it will long be a monument of learning which no educated Manxman will despise ; nor will Bishop Hildesley, under whom the scheme was carried out, be forgotten as the Bishop whose administration has not been surpassed in sacred usefulness.

The style of doctrine in those days may be inferred from the sermons of Bishop Wilson, usually taken as the ideal

THE ESTABLISHED CHURCH. 133

and representative minister of the Manx Church. His position was Protestant towards Romanism. In his teaching, there was a strict enforcement of the morals of Christianity, and the obligation of religious ordinances. To the question, " What must I do to be saved ? " his substantial answer was repentance and amendment of life, with the observance of the ordinances of the Church. The doctrine of faith in the atoning sacrifice of Christ as the condition of salvation was absent, and, as suggested by the Rev. Hugh Stowell, his first biographer, the system of evangelical truth was but imperfectly unfolded. He held Apostolical succession, priestly absolution, sacramental efficacy by virtue of administration by men episcopally ordained. He was an ideal Bishop with Keble, who remarked with approval that he had not in any of his writings recognised the necessity of sensible conversion and an assurance of present personal salvation. For denying the power of priestly absolution, he subjected one of his clergy to discipline. His peculiar views had their influence, probably in leaving his diocese during his long episcopate without the Scriptures in their own tongue. The congregations were left to the off-hand renderings into Manx of the English version in their sermons. Bishop Hildesley took a different view in securing the Manx Bible; he urged his clergy to the study and use of the language, and severely criticised those who deemed it a loss of respectability to know their native tongue. No doubt the prevalent native sentiment was that expressed by a woman in Lezayre, when her son read to her the Manx Scriptures for the first time, "We have sit in darkness until now."

The discipline of the Manx Established Church in its earlier days of reformation was severely oppressive. Its most marked example is found in Bishop Wilson's administration. He had obtained the sanction of the Legislature for his *Ecclesiastical Constitutions*, which were, in fact, a summary of Canon law, and by him they were strictly enforced by penance, by fine, by imprisonment, by dragging through the sea at the tail of a boat, officially provided by the Governor, by the threat of what would make eternity hopeless. There was penance for parents who did not teach their children the Church Catechism, for non-attendance at the Church services, for moral failure where civil law could not interfere. Marriage was denied those who were not confirmed. There was the white sheet of penance at Church or at the market place, varied by the fine, the dungeon, or the sea. More than once poor Kate Kinrade was doomed to the last. For refusal to carry out the Bishop's sentence on a Communicant, the Archdeacon was suspended from office and Benefice. For refusing the sum demanded for tithes the Clerk of the Rolls was sent to prison without permission of self-defence. The "Bridle" was in the care of the Sumner for those who failed to govern their tongue. The civil administration of law among the people seemed largely absorbed in the spiritual. At last the Governor refused to execute the sentences of the Bishop, the Earl of Derby accused him of invading his province, the Legislature repealed certain laws on which the Bishop had taken action, and, in the issue, the Bishop and his two Vicars-General were imprisoned in Castle Rushen, though this was disallowed on appeal to the English Government. The moral effect on the people gave the Bishop no satisfaction.

It causes wonder to see so noble a nature perverted by a mistaken system, as in the Bishop, and to see the approval of such methods by the poet of the Christian Year in his two volumes of biography. Relief must be sought in a more general view of his character. For, notwithstanding what has thus far come within view, he was a man of Christian humility, sincerity, and zeal. His faults were those of his

THE ESTABLISHED CHURCH.

age and of his creed and system. He refused promotion, and held to the humbler position, though royalty honoured him, and a leading statesman pronounced him an example of Apostolic times. But his fine, imperial nature was turned from the lines of Apostolic procedure by his wrong idea of duty. Apart from this, there is much to admire. He found Bishop's Court greatly tending to ruin, and changed it into a comely residence, planted its grounds with trees, and gave the farmers a model for imitation in farming their land. He was generous to the poor, the helper of education, restored churches by repairs, and added to their number, and laboured much in preaching and otherwise for the welfare of his diocese and for the Manx people. Had he, with all his other excellences, been in full possession of the evangelical system, how different would have been his power and success.

At first, the services of the Manx Church of the Reformation were chiefly, if not entirely, in Manx; in later times, partly; in the present, entirely English. The names of some who have held a place in its pulpit are still household words, not to name any yet living: Stowell, Howard, Brown, Cain, Drury. Few Sabbath scenes have been so finely suggestive, as in Braddan churchyard in the open-air service during "the season," with "Parson Drury" as the preacher, belonging to the age when there were giants in the earth, and certainly in excellence as well as in stature, commencing with Cowper's hymn, "There is a fountain filled with blood," etc.; the old church on the left; the wealth of memories from the graves; the rich frame of trees which have required ages for their growth; the listening crowd around, come from Douglas mostly, and drawn by a twofold beauty, that of the scene and of the service. He was also one of the few surviving masters of Manx. During the first thirty years of this century, the church service was often in

Manx, and Drury was to the manner born. I remember the difficulty of an Englishman with a Manx living, to whom a Manx curate was essential. An old Manx friend, who was present at the morning Manx service in Andreas, once told me of an attempt by the English clergyman, who had been studying Manx, to read the second lesson, Luke xv., but he failed in pronunciation. The Manx word for "fatted" is much like the word for "drowned" in pronunciation; "beight" (fatted), "baiht" (drowned). He failed in the shade of difference, and the result to the Manx ear of my friend was "bring hither the drowned calf," etc.

Compared to the last century, when the Established Church stood alone without any Nonconformists, the surroundings are materially different. The growth of a strong Nonconformity, the reduction of the rural population in the parishes, the new political and municipal life, the changes in popular opinions, have largely influenced the relative position of the Manx Church. Still, its social power is considerable, and its prestige peculiar as the State Church. Small and feeble as it is among the great dioceses of England, there has been an idea in higher quarters of blending it with one of them, but sentiments of nationality and antiquity have been too strong to allow the proposal to take effect.

The identity of a Church of the Reformation with the purer Church of the early ages, by the abandonment of the intermediate papal corruptions, is a curious question. The corruption, however, was absorption by the papal system, a change of essence—doctrine, ritual, spirit, government— another gospel, and the moral identity is lost. Succession is not identity. A race intermarrying with another is not the same in the after generations. A Socinian church in the lineal descent from the old Presbyterian is not the Church of the earlier age. If the river be pure from the temple to the Dead Sea, as in Ezekiel, the identity remains; but where other streams of a foul nature enter into the original stream, the identity is lost. There must be a return to the source. There must be a renewal. The true test of a Church is not found in agreement with any age, but in agreement with Scripture; not even external descent, if the theological and moral be corrupted. "I had planted thee a noble vine, wholly a right seed; how then art thou turned into the degenerate plant of a strange vine unto me?"

The clergy number about fifty-eight, of whom some twenty are Manx. In addition to the Bishop and Archdeacon there are four Canons.

Social Changes: Manx Methodism.

WESLEYAN CHAPEL, SULBY-GLEN, ISLE OF MAN.

CHAPTER XIV.

SOCIAL CHANGES: MANX METHODISM.

HE general view appropriate to these chapters as part of Manx history compels the omission of much valuable detail, and which may possibly be given in a small supplementary volume.

The Isle of Man is first named in Methodist history in Wesley's account of his first Conference in 1744, when the Rev. John Meriton, a clergyman from the Isle of Man, was present by invitation. Mr. Meriton had offered his services to Bishop Wilson for special evangelistic efforts on Sabbath evenings, but his offer had been declined on the ground that the earlier church services of the day were sufficient.

The moral condition of the Manx people towards the closing quarter of the eighteenth century was deeply degraded. The Rev. John Murlin, a Wesleyan minister resident in Whitehaven, then visited the Island, but found moral conditions so discouraging that he despaired of doing good and returned home, saying that the place was "a nest of smugglers." The lawlessness, which led in 1765 to the revestment of the Island in the Crown to secure better social order, was then triumphant. Bishop Wilson had recently passed away, with much disappointment in the results of his long episcopate. Moral teaching, without the great evangelical truths, though enforced by the penances of the Canon law, had failed to secure social regeneration; some popish habits still lingered; little could be said of the ministrations in the parish churches; there were no Sabbath schools. A letter from the Archbishop of York to Bishop Hildesley urged more attention to some prevalent evils among the clergy and in other forms. The moral state of the community was a new edition of "Jesus I know, and Paul I know, but who are ye?" It was an illustration of the moral disadvantage of a people largely without the Scriptures; for, in a population of 28,000, more than two-thirds knew only their own language, and there was no Manx Bible until 1772. The facilities for smuggling had led multitudes astray from all goodness; the loose laws of bankruptcy had helped other evils by attracting a considerable class of unprincipled debtors from England, with a dissolute expenditure. Still, it must be admitted that Mr. Murlin's despondency was excessive, for events soon proved that there was really a great opportunity of doing good.

The work of Manx Methodism began in 1775, when Mr. John Crook, a local preacher, was sent by the Methodists of Liverpool to preach and engage in Christian work. In the same year, under Wesley's sanction, he became the third Minister in the Whitehaven Circuit, to which the Island was allotted. His preaching soon attracted multitudes, and with much success. At Castletown the Governor and his lady and family, with some of the clergy, came to hear him preach, and received him with great kindness. Many were gathered into Christian fellowship, converts of gifts were trained for Christian work, and among them native local preachers of no common ability.

Until 1775 the Established Church stood alone, with its seventeen parish churches and three or four chapels-of-ease. It was said that there were no Nonconformists in the Island. But a change was quickly apparent. What might be termed a new reformation began with the labours of Crook. A religious revival swept over the land, and in a few years some

MANX METHODISM.

thousands of the Manx people were formed into Methodist Societies. On his first visit to the Island, in 1781, Wesley deemed the work to be one of the greatest Gospel successes known to him " in the three kingdoms." His visit moved the country. Landing at Douglas, after two days at sea from Whitehaven, he preached on the day of his arrival in the Douglas Market Place ; on successive days he preached to multitudes at Castletown, on the mountain of South Baroole, at Peel, Barregarrow, and Ballaugh, closing his week at Andreas and Ramsey. In his tour the Rector of Ballaugh, with his family, came to the service, and treated him with great cordiality. Wesley notes with satisfaction that he found no opposition from Governor or Bishop, or the bulk of the clergy. Already the Island had appointed to it two "travelling preachers." It was only nine years since the Manx people had come into possession of the Manx Scriptures.

The Christian motive of the Mission thus so successful was conspicuous. The distant sight of the Island from his Whitehaven Circuit had moved the sympathy of Mr. Murlin to cross and reconnoitre the fortress of darkness ; the zeal and ability of Liverpool Methodism provided for the effort ; the aim was simply scriptural holiness through the land, without a sectarian bias, and with the desire to help those who most needed the Gospel. The noble spirit was clearly recognised by the Governor, and by some of the clergy, who welcomed the evangelical effort.

The rapidity which marked the spread of Manx Methodism was striking. The island soon became an important "Circuit"; chapels were built, Sabbath schools opened, local preachers, with rich command of Manx, raised in great force; within the first ten years from 1775 the membership rose to 2,121; in 1798 to 4,840 in a population of 31,500. In later years, under stricter methods, the numerical returns have been reduced. The last returns show a membership, including probationers and juniors, of 3,163; ten ministers; 164 local preachers; 214 class leaders; the religious services each year, on the Sabbath, 6,932; on week nights, 2,248. The four Methodist Circuits include every town and village and parish and many scattered hamlets and districts, so as to cover the Island more or less with accommodation for worship, with Sunday Schools in proportion, and with Day Schools in the larger populations. The exact statistics are not within reach. Of late years some noble additions have been made by the erection of new churches. At first many of the religious services were in farmhouses and barns; now the island can bear comparison with England in its provision for worship in all that constitutes adaptation and architectural beauty. Leaving statistics for the results among the people, Methodism has become historic in many families in many generations; its beneficial influence may be traced in various branches in the old country, and in other lands; from solitary converts in early days may be noted sometimes, three or four generations back, groups of descended families of marked distinction in character and prosperity. Methodist traditions have a wide range among the population, whose ancestors were in Methodism, but who are themselves in other communions. The strength of Methodism is among the middle classes; farmers, merchants, shop-keepers, prosperous men of business in almost every line; not a few who, by good moral habits and industry, are on the verge of wealth; men who give their leisure to municipal affairs, or legislative in the House of Keys. It has done much to give reality to the Manx Reformation, and supremacy in the public mind to the doctrines of Christianity. The ritualistic and the rationalistic have but little influence. To multitudes, now for some generations, it has brought morality and godliness; to the community, a social order that can dispense with military control; to public opinion, health and what makes for righteousness. The results to a people and country must be valuable where a church widely extended, and for generations, has maintained some thousands in membership, and where evangelical pulpit-teaching, the culture of gifts for religious service, schools for Sabbath and week-day, and other forms of usefulness, have long helped to give "social evolution," in the highest sense of the expression. Its range of ministration includes the Island. It knows how to give as well as how to labour, and is generous in religious outlay; within the last few years, in Douglas alone, from £15,000 to a much higher figure has been spent in church and school extension, while in other towns and in some of the villages kindred efforts have been made.

The means of this extension has been the simple ministration of the Gospel. Under the divine blessing, the Manx mind was early possessed by Manx preaching; the English ministry, in successive appointments, has nobly led on the work; the lay preaching has been above what is often found, the type of doctrinal truth has been that of the early days, without modern fashion; the whole machinery of the Church has been in action, with readiness for service in many workers; steady loyalty has been maintained to constitutional standards; and the result is a Manx Methodism of true stability and power in the best interests of the people.

Such results, however, have not been arrived at without severe persecution in the earlier stages, and social antagonism, sometimes from the populace, sometimes from the clergy led on by the Bishop. As elsewhere, the early Methodists were driven from the Lord's table in the parish churches. The parson of the parish sometimes headed the popular rage. In Douglas, the clergyman of the old Chapel, Master of the Grammar School, and Rector of Bride as well, became prominent with his boys in riotous disturbance. Bishop Richmond, in the year after Methodism began its Manx mission, issued a letter to be read in all the parish churches, denouncing the Methodists in their meetings, and their teachers as profane and blasphemous pretenders to religion. Conscious of his power under the " Ecclesiastical Constitutions," he demanded the names of all who attended the Methodist services, so taking the first step towards the infliction of penance, with its fines and imprisonments in the dungeon of the " moddey dhoo," and beyond, excommunication and perdition, as the priesthood might adjudge. The Methodists of Douglas, in attending their religious services, were hooted and stoned by the mob ; the pupils of the Grammar School, encouraged by their master, assailed Mr. Crook with stones and filth as he passed along the street. It is pleasant to add in contrast that a later Bishop (Mason) was of a different type, and showed a tolerant and friendly spirit.

But, notwithstanding opposition, Methodism continued to prosper. In Douglas, in 1801, was begun the first Sunday School in the Island, in connection with the chapel ; new chapels were erected in various parts, while persecution still raged generally, but especially in Baldwin, Marown, Peel, and Ramsey. It was a continuance of the spirit of Bishop Barrow, in the time of Charles II., who made him both Bishop and Governer, when, with historic severity, he oppressed the Nonconformists of his time and claimed all the Manx people as belonging exclusively to the Established Church.

The stability of Manx Methodism, without resources external to itself except the divine, is a useful study. The great feature has been evangelical preaching and evangelical Church life. Venerated names, now historic for such a ministry, will arise in the Manx memory—Mercer, and many since who have passed from earth. Theirs was preaching which did not hesitate to speak of eternal sanctions, and which, with no reading from the complete pulpit manuscript, freely declared the whole counsel of God, and unencumbered by critical reserve. This was true of the labourers in the vineyard then, and is true still of the local preachers as well as the ministers. The strong body of lay workers is a chief reason of the stability now in view. Wesley was filled with admiration of the local preachers ; he had not seen " so many stout, well-looking " men of that order together. But six years after the beginning of the work there were twenty-two local preachers. For the first thirty years the number averaged 100 ; the number in 1893 was 153. A Church membership yielding so large a proportion of preachers must hold a good level of culture and Christian zeal. In the present volume space will not allow detail ; but there was a group of these men who will not soon be forgotten : Faragher of Cooilcam, Cowley, known as "Iliam e Close," Ellison, Stephen, Lace, Sayle, Kneale, among others, men of original gifts, and of much usefulness in the early age. Between the ministers and the local preachers there was, for an interval including 1835, one who was neither Circuit minister nor local preacher in the usual sense, and whose name on the "plan" was between the two—the late Rev. Robert Aitken, whose ministry gave an interval of peculiar interest and power. Secondary events must here be omitted, but his wonderful ministry may be recorded. For moving eloquence, for preaching effectiveness, his equal has been seldom seen in the pulpit ; tall, commanding, earnest, the voice ranging from the tender to the terrific ; the reading of the hymn equal to many a sermon in congregational effect; the text, perhaps, peculiar; the sermon showing the man of the University and the true evangelist the usefulness corresponding.

There were also visits of eminent ministers from England, who added much to the intellectual life and stability of Manx Methodism. The insular feeling was thus saved from narrowness, and raised into a higher sphere. When Samuel Leigh came from New Zealand to a meeting in Douglas, the man of missionary heroism; when the eloquence of Robert Wood—then young—awoke from the free seats the exclamation, " Dear me, what a man that is ! "; when Gideon Ouseley related his Irish experiences ; when J. B. Gillman, Irishman at once in oratory and physique, rose to the height of his argument; when Newton, Beaumont, Lessay, Macafee, and others of those days, dealt grandly with their theme, it was an education to the Manx Methodist, it broke in on Manx isolation, and was something like the call to come out from the seclusion of the tent to gaze at the stars of heaven.

Among the reasons of stability was the style of the early preaching. In such style each age has its peculiarity. In this case the preaching would not now be considered " up to the times," but it proved itself to be up to the Gospel and to the great interests of humanity. Its success made evident the order of its excellence. In its best type it resembled the island in which it had its sphere, but with none of the mists of " manninan MacLear "; fixed in the gulf stream of redemption, clear in outline, with fields rich in beauty, with something to remind of Snaefell in its grandeur; here a rocky headland, there a receding bay, with a light on the great points of danger, with a final shelter within defences never to be shaken ; while beyond was the unfathomed ocean from the equator to the poles. At all events the preaching was mighty, and led to great religious revivals, which were another sign of the stability mentioned.

Another consideration entered largely into this matter: Manx Methodism has maintained its specific peculiarities in their fulness. It has not abandoned, not lowered, the class meeting, the lovefeast, the prayer meeting. It has been too old-fashioned to eliminate its peculiarities on the plea of catholicity. The reason for the existence of a church or system of any other kind is to be found in its peculiarities, as also the secret of its power. It is in them you find the reason for being a Methodist rather than a member of some other Church. Organic unity obtained by the surrender of specific differences is a loss. Abandon what is peculiar to the British constitution, and what remains worthy of England? The great excellence, of which all else is the basis, is in the specific difference rather than the genus, as the logician would contend. It is in the secluded regions, often, that things longest retain the grand old type; and the sea that rolls around Manxland is one reason why it is so conservative of the initial and early forms of life in the Church and in other ways.

It should be added that the relations of Methodism to the Established Church have been friendly and catholic, though nonconformist. In the early times, as elsewhere, the two were not so distinct and separate. The services were not so often held in church hours; the Methodists went to church, the churchmen attended the chapel. At the same time, there was a separate organisation. But, on both sides, things have tended to change. Methodists were sometimes driven from the sacramental table in the parish churches. The doctrines preached were not always evangelical. The Methodists have realised their economy as of providential origin, and as a Scriptural Church in all essentials of doctrine, order, discipline, and economy. In so doing, they own to no schism; the membership has not been drawn from religious fellowship in some other Church, but from the world. It does not allow the State the function of deciding to what Church a man must belong. It does not admit the exclusive claims of any other communion. The notions of "Apostolic Succession," of priestly power of absolution, of sacramental efficiency apart from personal penitence and faith, are no part of their creed. They hold the maxim at the same time that they are the friends of all, the enemies of none, and, meanwhile, look to their own ministers for religious ordinances and services, and not elsewhere. In all this question, their general position rests on the principles of Wesley himself. His final aim was Scriptural holiness through the land. His view was that, church or no church, souls must be saved, the order of his Church must give way to usefulness in the course of Providence. He held the Anglican idea of Apostolic Succession to be unproved, and denied it; further, that Presbyters and Bishops were the same order in the New Testament; that as a presbyter he had the power of ministerial ordination equally with any bishop. He ordained men to the Christian ministry for the United Kingdom, and for the United States of America. He refused the jurisdiction of the Bishops of the Established Church. He disregarded parochial boundaries, saying that the world was his parish. His lines of procedure extended have led to the greater distance from the Church of England line, but the angle of departure has been under the guidance of Wesley's example. As a Christian, he was consistent; as a Churchman, he refused to give absolute submission.

Wesleyan Methodism does not now stand alone as the only Nonconformist Church in Man. About 1810, was built the church of "Parson Haining," now succeeded by the Congregational Church in Prospect Hill ; on the Castletown Road was the Romanist Chapel, with its successor also in Prospect Hill ; since, about 1823, has risen the large membership of the Primitive Methodists ; later still, the Methodist New Connexion has taken its place in the island. Presbyterian Churches have also been formed in Douglas and Ramsey; the Salvation Army also has done good service. These form the group of evangelical Nonconformist Churches in the Island, so far as I know. I will only add that the tendency to closer fellowship and brotherly feeling among the ministers and people of these Churches is to be hailed as one of the happiest signs of the times.

Summary and Review.

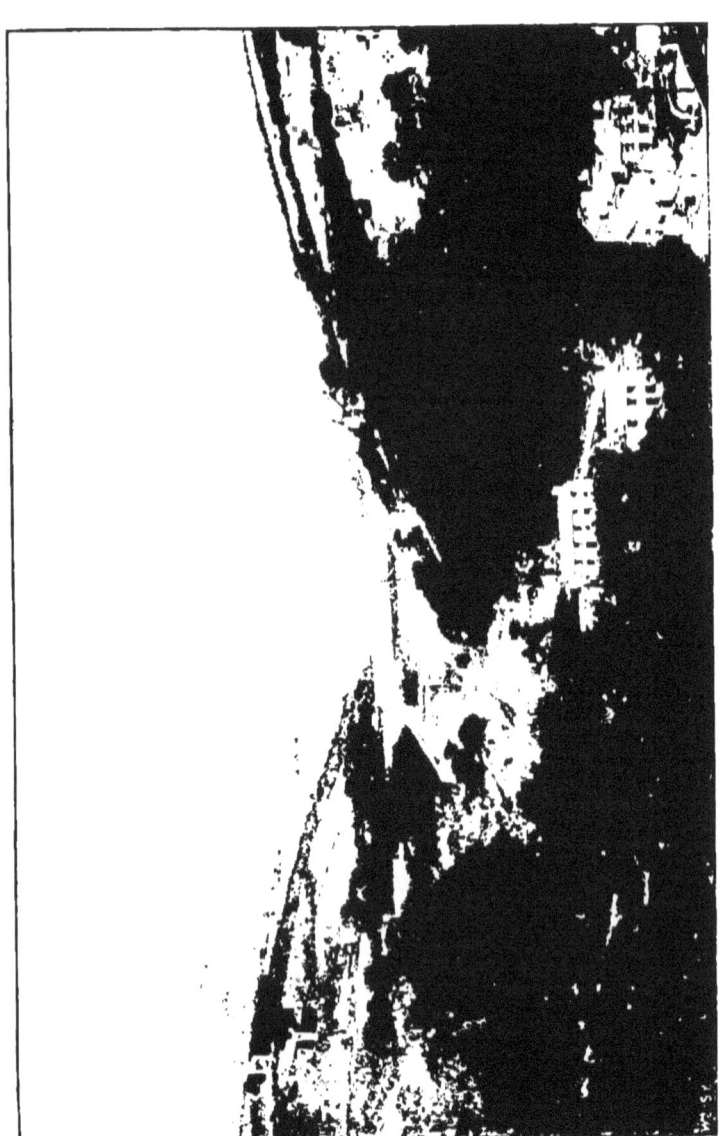

LAXEY GLEN.

CHAPTER XV.

SUMMARY AND REVIEW.

O place me in some Heaven-protected Isle,
Where Peace and Equity and Freedom smile,
Where no volcano pours its fiery flood,
No crested warrior dips his plume in blood;
Where Power secures what Industry has won,
Where to succeed is not to be undone;
A land with sea and mountain, rock and plain,
In Mona's Isle beneath Victoria's reign.
(Adapted from Couper.)

A BRIEF summary and review may be a useful close of the foregoing chapters in relation to Manx progress, past and future.

Until 1703, Manx civilisation had made but little progress in all the centuries. The transition from Popery threw off Papal supremacy, and made the Manx Church a separate organisation. But it did not bring material social advance; the same Bishop remained, the same priesthood, the same intolerance in religion, the same political despotism. The term Protestant, as descriptive, meant only a protest against Papal supremacy. The immediate doctrinal change was slight; canon law was still supreme. The essential elements of civilised progress were wanting; no general education worthy of the name, no moral life to mark Manx history, no advance in agriculture and commerce. On the question of agriculture, the land had been falling out of cultivation ever since the usurpation of the ownership by the Earl of Derby in 1643. As to insular revenue, it was trifling. As to freedom, there was no political enfranchisement. The Act of Settlement itself, for a time, bore but little fruit beyone public contentment with the restitution. In the Revestment of the Island in the British Crown, in 1765, there was much provisional power of progress. The two acts were the chief points around which a true policy might be successful ; but the civilisation thus far was only humble in its order, both as to the people and as to their outward condition. Of Christian civilisation at the time little can be said. The distinctive doctrine of the English and European Reformation was in abeyance ; socially, there was the blight of smuggling on a scale which visibly injured the Imperial Exchequer ; the dishonest resources of English bankrupts, sheltered from their creditors by Manx law, brought a temporary but demoralising prosperity until the repeal of the law in 1814. Throughout the Island mobs were ready to assail serious people on their way to worship. There was no adequate guarantee against social violence. It was thus towards the end of last century.

The seeds of a better condition had been sown in the religious revival of the last quarter of that century, amid the ministrations of Protestant truth, and a great moral improvement among multitudes, of whom many were gathered into Christian fellowship. In this great movement lay the promise of the future in social elevation.

The great opportunity for commercial development has been the rank of the Island as a chief watering-place in the United Kingdom, with the disadvantages and the advantages of the sea around it for storm as well as calm. From this comes the material progress of this century ; hence the noble fleet of steamships belonging to the Isle of Man Steam Packet Company, the steamer between Peel and

Ireland (the whole yielding a passenger tax yearly of £2,695; arrivals and departures, 581,294), the piers and promenades, the hotels and lodging-houses, the market for the farm produce in garden and farmyard, the increased value of land, the new impulse given to water and gas companies, the opening for new and prosperous banks, and much more that adds to the enterprise of business life. Its special feature and success will be found in this supreme characteristic. The social state was thus created from which the political and municipal franchise could no longer be withheld. The Island could not be a place for great manufactures or great commerce; its mine of wealth is the modern passion for a yearly visit to the seaside, with its rest and recreation.

It is obvious that the conditions of successful competition with other great watering-places must be observed. In all such places moral respectability and good public order are essential; of such conditions the authorities of the Island are carefully observant, and Manx public opinion will not fail to sustain them in action. The "rowdy" element is fatal to the highest order of prosperity in such spheres. The respectable middle class, with their young people, are repelled by any approach to public disorder on week nights, and yet more on the Sabbath, by the open oyster and tobacco shops, by boating on the sea and such practices, and by the so-called sacred concert. The people of these tastes are not the class to be a source of wealth in the "season." It would not be commercial wisdom to adapt public arrangements to these, rather than to a standard which will do justice to all, whatever their individual preferences. The great watering places show a sagacious vigilance on these lines. From the first, the Isle of Man Steam Packet Company has been an example in refusing to sail its steamers on the Sabbath. The principles of good moral order are worth money in these public interests, to say nothing of what is higher : attractions to the best customers are increased.

The local improvements increase this successful competition. In this view, much has been done, and the same enterprise continues. Provision is in course for easy access to the beauties of Manx scenery not so near at hand. The electric tram gives ready access to the grand scenes and summit of Snaefell, while it has also opened out the beauties of Groudle and other recesses. The marine drive does similar service round Douglas Head. There are similar improvements elsewhere. Were it possible to attract, as in some places, visitors to spend their winter in the Island, a great addition would be made to Manx prosperity. One thing helpful to insular advantage is much needed, namely, a Nonconformist College with its provision of the higher education of Manx youth and others who are of non-established churches, just as King William's College meets the wants of the Established Church. Such a provision would possibly draw many to reside in Man.

In the spirited local improvements projected, there may be some fear of too high a charge for rates, and such increase would of course, by increasing the cost of living, be a disadvantage, especially if the result were to make Manx residences as costly as English. The principle includes much more, and successful competition will require all care in giving it practical effect. To such considerations, the people of the Island will not be insensible, from common business prudence, while reputation for kindness of manner and firmness in dealing stands deservedly high.

This review of the whole subject of the preceding chapters would be incomplete, if the religious history of the Island within the last century were not duly combined with the other parts of the subject. The commercial considerations named have their place, but what gives to the Island its special and distinctive social character arises from the prevalence of religious and moral principles among the population.

THE END.

www.ingramcontent.com/pod-product-compliance
Lightning Source LLC
Chambersburg PA
CBHW030308170426
43202CB00009B/917